REVIVED & RENOVATED

Real Life Conversations on the
Intersection of *Home, Faith* and
Everything in Between

VICTORIA DUERSTOCK
& PAIGE RIEN

Library of Congress Control Number: 2021943144
ISBN: 978-1-63797-008-9
eBook ISBN: 978-1-63797-009-6

Cover Design by Greg Jackson, Thinkpen Design
Interior design by Typewriter Creative Co.

Printed in India
TPL
10 9 8 7 6 5 4 3 2 1

For the "Women of Wonder Bread," my dear friends, and their gift of friendship, which revives & restores me, daily. —Paige

For our readers, whether newcomers or old friends, who seek encouragement in this season of building and rebuilding. —Victoria

CONTENTS

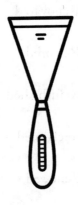

Dear Reader,

Welcome to *Revived and Renovated!* We're so happy to invite you into our conversations. We were simply amazed to find the rich opportunities to explore the meaning of all these home improvement, renovation and decor words and their dual meanings in scripture and the language of our faith.

We are both wives and mothers, we both write and create for a living, both of us love anything to do with creating a home. But we are not in the same place—one of us is from Mississippi, one of us is from Maryland—we have quite different stories and journeys to God as you'll soon see in our conversations. We bring different experiences, traditions and language to the table here, but find common ground in our love for the Lord, our deep gratitude for what He has done in our lives, and our excitement with just how much the work of homemaking is like the Lord's work on *us*. Sometimes, it's a big job and everything needs to be gutted, sometimes, it's a simple refresh. And as we both love old houses, and believe strongly that everyone is redeemable, there is no such thing as a tear-down!

We want you to know that you are invited into this conversation whether you have long been devoted to a life of faith or whether you are still unsure about God. We know that many of you have painful stories, and some may be in pain even today. You are most welcome wherever you are. If you are curious as to whose voice you are reading along the way, you'll find Victoria's comments justified to the left margin and Paige's to the right.

Additionally, throughout the book you'll find "Real Projects to Progress in the Home." These simple ideas from Paige will help you get started and move forward.

We hope and pray this book blesses your life and home and all those you encounter!

Victoria & Paige

I will restore to you the years that the swarming locust has eaten, the hopper, the destroyer, and the cutter, my great army, which I sent among you. "You shall eat in plenty and be satisfied, and praise the name of the Lord your God, who has dealt wondrously with you. And my people shall never again be put to shame.

Joel 2:25-26

Chapter 1

REVIVED

revived[1]: /ri-viv-d/ *adjective*

1: regarding a person or thing that's been restored to consciousness of life, or from a depressed, inactive or unused state: brought back

2: renewed in the mind or memory

The concept of being revived is essential and a great place to begin our conversations. Bringing something back to life for the home is such a satisfying process, whether it's a piece of furniture we found by the side of the road, or a family heirloom long forgotten. And God's hand reviving us is no different; like water to a sun-parched spirit, revival activates us once again, causing us to move forward. Let us begin!

To me, this definition describes going from not doing anything to doing something, to begin, to start, to take

---

1 www.merriam-webster.com/dictionary/revive

that first step. And I think it's a good starting point on this journey. For someone who is stuck, whether in the home, their personal life, their relationships, or habits—just taking the first tiny step is actually *reviving*.

In our modern life, with social media and so much perfection, whether it's in the home or in the spiritual life, we can think, "I'm so far from that, I don't know where to begin." But to revive is not necessarily attaining that Instagram perfection, but to take the first step in the direction of what *your* version of that is. And we don't talk about that enough; that the beginning is just one small step.

We talk about this a lot when we're having conversations about forming habits, just trying to get things done around the house like chores and the like, and being revived, and coming back to life again. Sometimes a cool drink of water on a hot day is enough to get us going to the next step.

It doesn't complete anything, it doesn't finish anything, but it does get us started. And I love that idea of activation because it is important how we how think about being revived in our homes. As a designer, what do you see as a need for reviving things we already have or our spaces? I know you've played around your own spaces lately with how they're being used, you've brought new life back to them, right? Because when something's not being used, it needs to find new life.

Well, I'm going to borrow from my first church, which was the 12 steps of AA[2], and I'm going to just borrow my favorite

---

2 Alcoholics Anonymous

phrase from the whole program, which is "next right action." And that's something we'll get into as we go along. I've been in recovery for a long time, but the phrase, "next right action" is something I come back to in every facet of my life when something isn't working, and I feel stuck. It doesn't say, *get to the rearranging of the furniture* or *make the addition happen* or even *clean up the whole room*, which maybe looks like a bomb hit it. It says, next right action, which, as you said, is sometimes just having glass of water.

Sometimes it's calling a friend, sometimes it's making a list. Actually, even before that, I would say acceptance of whatever the situation is, is a good action to take. Acceptance is the first step as we say in the program! *OK, now I need to accept that this is not working.* And then what is the action after that?

Plead my cause and redeem me; give me life according to your promise!

Psalm 119:154

In our home, we had a formal living room and three sons that seemed to get bigger overnight. We're all big and boisterous, and here I had this posh, formal space with lots of breakables and glass coffee tables. And I did love it, but it just didn't work with the season we were in, or the children God gave us! First, I thought to myself, "I need that room for something else"—it wasn't really getting used as a formal space.

Second, at any time they might demolish it in five minutes! We just needed that room to be something else entirely. And so, we've made it into a space we needed for the kids—fun, casual, playful. But it wasn't by a snap of the fingers. The first thing was an admission, *OK, this is not working.* Then the next right action was getting rid of some stuff, writing down a plan, and evaluating what the room needed.

So, I know we get very overwhelmed, but the question isn't "how to get it done?" It's really, "what is the first action and then the next right one?" I can't buy it all today or move it all at once. We have physical and financial limitations. The next right action is sometimes taking a breath, and just deciding a change is needed, which seems both monumental, and bite-sized, if you will.

I love it and I love that you accepted the season you were in with your boys and your family and said, "how can my home be functional and still work for me in a beautiful way?" Because is it form or is it function? That's always an interesting conversation when it comes to our design and how we do things.

But I think it is both, right? It needs to function, and have some sense to it, but it needs to be beautiful as well, because we all desire beautiful spaces, and everyone's definition of beauty is different. You know that whole revived idea works in our personal lives as well. No matter how long you've been on your faith journey, there are dry seasons where you're in the desert and you maybe feel like the Lord's been silent for a long time.

I know that even in this Covid journey we have all seen this big change in our lives. And I know that there has been a season of dryness just because it's been different and everything that was normal is no longer normal.

I think that breathing new life is also so important in a season after you've been through something really dry or even defeating. Death, loss, all those things come to mind when I think of that restart—the whole bringing back to life. So, I love the idea of just digging into how we can talk about being revived again, especially our spirits.

Well, my mind's buzzing, Victoria, because I'm thinking about my living room and I'm also now thinking about the Resurrection! And I'm thinking about how God *really* wants full restoration for us and sometimes we have to ask God to revive us and to revive the situation. We're in a situation now where we're coming out of this lockdown, still in some form of quarantine, and things are starting to perk up again. But my prayer is often: "Lord, tell me which direction to go, because everybody is doing it differently."

And that's true in anything, right? Everybody organizes their home in different ways, and everybody does this walking back into life differently. Another prayer of mine is "Lord, show me how to restart. Tell me the first action to take. Tell me what's safe. Tell me what my next move should be." But I think that's what God wants for us. And He wants full restoration, and He wants a full life for us. In fairness it just looks different every season and for every family.

And there's the whole idea of the Resurrection as the cornerstone of faith in general. We believe that the resurrection is pivotal to everything that we put our faith in. As part of that revival, a favorite hymn I had growing up was called, "Revive Us Again." The title reminds me it's not once and done. Sometimes we need it more than one time as we go through those seasons, through those times, and through heartaches where we just don't understand. It's after that we need to be rebooted, right? Just relaunched—there's still something out there for me. There's still something out there for you. There's still something out there even after the hard times and the dark days. And I think that that's the message of being revived.

> That's beautiful. It is daily bread, after all, right? It is a daily revival. I forget that a lot, too, because I want to arrive and never need to lean on God again or never face my weaknesses again. But that is really our daily struggle. And the beauty of getting older is that you realize that daily dependence is how it works, and it's OK.

That is the beauty of getting older because we do have that perspective—it really is the journey. It's not really in the arrival where we can find that beauty.

> One thing that popped into my mind, and I think this relates to our journey with God and also our journey in the home, is that willingness is the fuel we need to start that engine. So, if we're trying to revive something that's dead, it not going to happen out of thin air. And sometimes there's a real need for prayers of willingness. "Please let me be willing, Lord, to declutter a space or put some stuff on Facebook marketplace to sell or talk to my spouse about changing a room around."

Or "Please give me the willingness to get on my knees and pray in the morning or find my Bible or call that faithful friend and connect." Sometimes we don't realize we need that fuel. And I don't always pray for the thing. I pray for the willingness to do the thing, right?

I love that you went there Paige because that is important. We have to be willing to do the work and then watch Him do the work within us. It's really both, not either/or.

What about you? Do you feel that desire in your spirit for a revival of sorts? Our prayer is that you will turn to your Bibles, dig in and just start right there where you are. And if you have a hard time starting, that you'll simply pray for God to help you begin. (Because He will.) You're not going to make a mistake. We know the power of God's Word and we know it will absolutely overflow into your home—and it begins with one small step.

Will you not revive us again, that your people may rejoice in you?

—Psalm 85:6 NIV

REFURBISH WORKSHOP

take stock and see all the options before you

Occasionally we are clear that we don't like something, but we can't move forward until we analyze all the possibilities for renewing a piece. This is a workshop to think through the options with that piece of furniture you don't want to get rid of and prefer to remake. This is about seeing a piece with all its individual components—the pieces that work together to make the whole. Imagine the piece with parts removed or replaced. Think through the possibilities of small and/or big changes. It's easy to visualize painting an object, but what about breaking it down and refurbishing it with different materials? Here are some questions for your analysis:

- What would it be like if you replaced the hardware—hinges, pulls, handles? Or added hardware where there is none? (Yes, you can do that.) Or simply moved the location of the hardware?

- What would it be like if you removed the drawers or doors? Can what is now a dresser or an armoire become open shelving or storage?

- If it's a table, can the legs be shortened to be used as a table for children or a coffee table?

- What if the solid doors were replaced with glass?
- What if the tabletop was replaced with marble? Or copper?
- Thinking about paint—could you paint just one part, say the exterior—and leave part of the piece bare wood? What would it look like if you painted the whole thing?

Product tip: I'm very fond of changing hardware but this is tricky when you have a set of holes from the old components. You could replace them with the same size/shape of hardware. Or you could fill the holes with wood putty, sand them down once dry, and then paint over the repairs so you can relocate the hardware as necessary. Wood putty is inexpensive and sold in hardware stores.

There are so very many kinds of paint. New paint products are being developed all the time and your local independently owned paint store has a wealth of knowledge to share! Typically, these folks aren't knowledgeable about chalk paints and furniture-refinish products, however. Chalk Paint is easy to use but does not leave you with a hard, hearty finish, which I am always thinking about with kids. I prefer Benjamin Moore Advance Paint for furniture projects, but it takes practice and is more expensive. If you're just starting out, Chalk Paint is a great way to learn. It's forgiving if you mess up and less toxic so you can work on pieces near small children or animals. Good luck!

Chapter 2

RENOVATED

renovated: /REN-uh-vaytd/ *adjective*

regarding a person, place or space that's been restored to a former, better state (as by cleaning, repairing or rebuilding) or restored to life, vigor, or activity.[1]

We tend to think of renovations as big projects to the home, but renovations come in all shapes and sizes. Sometimes more substantial work is required to make a house better, but sometimes all that's required or possible is a deep clean and good paint job. God's work in us is no different—at times it's earth-shattering, other times it's more subtle and gentle. And when we are the house being renovated, we can rest in great trust: The Lord will fight for you; you need only to be still. Exodus 14:14 NIV

This is a big one! I doubt there's anyone in America right now that hasn't thought about renovating their home. But

---

1   www.merriam-webster.com/dictionary/renovate

looking at that definition, there's more than meets the eye
here with this word, isn't there?

There has been kind of this resurgence of renovating and
refurbishing and all the restoration type work that's being
done right now in our homes. And then when you think
about renovating our hearts, what does that really look like?

Merriam-Webster says that to renovate is to "restore to a
better state." And I love that because in the home business
we're always saying to ourselves, "what is the state of the thing
or the house?" Is it in good condition? Does it need a total
overhaul? If you're buying vintage furniture, you're analyzing
the state of the thing from multiple angles and looking at
imperfections. You're considering, "is this acceptable to me?"
We always start in discernment.

For my purposes, normally I don't want pristine—I want to
make it my own. Lord knows I have had a lot of fun making
things into something else or giving them a *new state,*
if you will.

That's right! I think that's one of your unique gifts and
talents—finding ways to take things that exist and making
them better because you renovate them. You renovate a space
and make it better and you take items and renovate them.
You really do love the thrifting game.

I do, and it is most certainly a game!

And you love collecting items that have seen different uses in
life than they're being used for now, especially if they're on

the shelf at Goodwill or in a thrift store. Talk about why you love that so much. Why does that matter?

I'm very drawn to previous time periods—give me something mid-century-modern, give me something Victorian—I love them all. But I'm not a purist, so I may buy something old and then spray paint it green. I've been in some pretty hot debates with people over what can and can't be painted. Somebody will post a piece of furniture on social media and say, "What should I do with this?" And I'll say, "Paint it! Paint it purple, paint it red, paint it black, or paint it white!" Then people will comment, "NO! No, don't do that to this beautiful wood." I understand that response, but my feeling is that once it's *yours* and you want to renovate it, that's really your business. Now, would I take an antique in pristine condition, worth thousands, and spray-paint it yellow? Maybe not. But no promises!

> *Repent therefore, and turn again, that your sins may be blotted out, that times of refreshing may come from the presence of the Lord, and that he may send the Christ appointed for you, Jesus, whom heaven must receive until the time for restoring all the things about which God spoke by the mouth of his holy prophets long ago.*
>
> *Acts 3:19-21*

There's something to be said for putting the elbow grease into our homes and making something new. That is to me a very healing medicine, if you will, and a great use of my

mind and my hands. And I love that process. So anyway,
I'm pro-paint.

I love it. I think it's important to consider why we should
renovate instead of replace. I mean, what is it about our culture
in general that seems to toss items when they are no longer
useful? I think it's easier to replace than it is to renovate
as we just mentioned, the renovation means work, right? It
means putting in the time and effort and elbow grease and
some paint, like you said. So why? Why is replacing easier
than renovating?

Well, this has been on my mind and heart for a while because
our throwaway culture bothers me so much. We see it with
real estate, in consumer goods—we see it all over. In previous
generations, people purchased furniture *once*. Today, furniture
is getting less expensive, made with cheaper materials or
manufacturing methods, and I'm seeing more and more self-
assembled furniture as well. Therefore, it's inexpensive to
buy new with very little elbow grease, if you will.

Unless you're buying from IKEA! You need plenty of
instructions to assemble all those pieces!

Oh yes, we are no strangers to Swedish DIY! And now there
are companies that sell big pieces of furniture—sectionals you
assemble yourself from thousands of small pieces—making
IKEA look like kindergarten blocks. I think affordable
furniture is great, *but* if a piece of furniture has made it to
the thrift store or the Goodwill, it has a *story*. It's got some
miles on it if it's made it *that* far, and it's probably built to
last. IKEA stuff won't find its way to an estate sale. It's also

giving us the ability to compose our home without waiting. Previous generations have said, "I'm going to wait and save up to buy nice things." Now we don't have to wait—we can buy used or renovate something we find along the way. I can use skills instead of a big investment, and it offers a kind of freedom, which I think is wonderful.

I'm glad that you brought this idea into the whole process of renovation. Also, when you look at the work it takes inside of us—we don't arrive on earth perfect, we don't live our lives perfectly along the way. There are times that stretch us and mold us. We are not the same thinkers in our 40s that we were in our 20s, so there is some renovation that goes on inside us as well.

I just love the idea of there still being value—for furniture or for ourselves. And in my experience, our personal history is important. The story's still important in our lives as well. And yet there still needs to be this renovation process. And that's exactly what I see the Lord does in our hearts. He is renovating us in His image, right, because we are not anything like Him on a regular daily basis. I'm sinful, we're all sinful. We think things that we shouldn't think, we do things we shouldn't do. And yet He is constantly working in us as believers. He is constantly at work. Being reminded of that renovation idea inside of us as well is valuable.

Yes...I love that. Still valuable—I sure hope so! And at this point I'm not trying to restore my 25-year-old self; it's not even possible.

That ship has sailed!

And I'm not really that interested either! For me 25 wasn't that great, so, looking forward, my internal renovation is about embracing what all the years behind me have meant, and not always trying to "get back" to some earlier time. It's about owning our story and moving forward. I feel passionate about really facing our stories; there is such richness there. It's our job to look at it and feel comfortable in it, or suffer through the looking because some of our stories are extremely hard. But God is with us in every moment. He was with you in the story, and He is with you in every moment of healing from the stories. And He doesn't want us to close the book and put it away, but perhaps offer our healing for the benefit of another.

It's amazing that we're not even in the same state and yet I was just thinking, you know, that's the value of our stories too. The value is in the sharing and vulnerability that happens when we're honest with each other and say, "you know, I don't have it figured out" or "I don't know what I'm doing" or "I need help!" Just that admission many times pulls those masks off and allows us to be vulnerable with one another. And that's how relationships are built, on that basis of, you know what, I don't have it all together, but I hope you like me anyway.

I've been thinking about vulnerability too. It's hard for us, especially as women. We're supposed to roll out of bed, perfectly made up, ready to go!

We're supposed to be SuperMom! Do it all with a cupcake too!

And a smile! Ready for anything...There is just so much mask wearing. Finding a way to being vulnerable and who we really are is so important. But we persist in thinking everyone has things figured out and maybe we're the only ones who don't have certain things sorted through. Someone very dear to me would always remind me that "nobody has it licked."We look at people's outsides and we think we know the whole picture, but we don't. We see certain strengths and we think we know someone's story, but we don't. The reality is change is slow. We have to trust God and that "the work" we're putting in on ourselves is working. Unfortunately, I don't see the change in myself the way I see a change in, for instance, painting a desk! Much, much slower and more gradual.

I think that's an interesting connection to the home, though. You think about renovating—in a lot of these homes that are being renovated they take off the drywall and see the brick underneath—this beautiful brick. It's exposed, right? Exposing something that was underneath. And sometimes that process is scary and sometimes you don't know what you're going to get. This is just amazingly beautiful because what was underneath was actually prettier than what was behind "the mask." And I think that's so beautiful for us to wrap up. Renovation can actually expose beauty versus more difficulty. Many times, there is more beauty underneath because it does make us real and honest and beautiful to each other.

Oh, my gosh, I love that. Taking off the mask allows us to be in real relationships. If you're wearing a mask there is only so much connection you can create. Even in this strange time that we find ourselves in, in the world, being bare, honest and vulnerable with how I am doing with a friend is very healing. Often the friend will say, "yeah, me too, I'm struggling also" or "oh yes, my anxiety is through the roof too." Sometimes we get into the mindset "maybe it's just me" that's struggling to keep it together or to stay positive or to remain hopeful. But the sharing of our hearts—even our darkness, is so important. Fellowship is sort of the glue, or if you will, the screws? What's the right building materials metaphor here? Is it the energy? I don't know. It's something that helps that renovation of the self. Maybe fellowship is the pit crew, I'm grasping at straws, but I know holy friends are important!

What a great way to wrap it up with our glue and pit crew—renovation is something so many of us long for. Renovation in our homes and again, for our hearts, is really done in community. Do you have a friend you can talk to about the renovation within? Many times, God's renovation in us is guided by holy friendship. May you find yours.

I am making all things new.

—Revelation 21:5 NASB

*Do not be conformed to this world,
but be transformed by the renewal of
your mind, that by testing you may
discern what is the will of God, what
is good and acceptable and perfect.*

Romans 12:2

Chapter 3

RESTORED

restored: /ri-stored/ *adjective*

regarding something or someone that has been given back, returned, or brought back into existence or use, brought back into a former state[1]

It's been said there are two kinds of people: old house lovers and everyone else. And for the most part, old house lovers have a deep desire to restore what is old and make it fresh and new again, being sure to celebrate the original beauty, charm and details. Restoration isn't reinvention. No tear downs, no starting over. Surely God works this way as well. So much of our work with God is a return—to old wounds and to His word and to the original promises to His people. Even just sitting and contemplating this is restorative to the weary.

There are so many nuances of the word restored. While it is similar to some of the words we have already discussed, it's

---

1   www.mirriam-webster.com/dictionary/restore

exciting to scratch the surface a bit and dig deeper to what might be just below the surface, because restore is its own special word.

> I love this word. As I was growing up, this was the first word in the design and home world that really hooked me. My parents took us to Williamsburg, Virginia, for a vacation when I was younger, and for the first time I saw old, restored spaces and things, and I thought, *wow, this is like being part of history.* This is connecting us "old souls" to a different moment in time. There's something so beautiful and romantic about that. And then I started to hear the word *restoration* in terms of our walk with God and it began to have even more resonance—all the work to make us whole again.

Yes. Because things take work that we want to keep using. We must restore things because a lot of times they become neglected.

> Yes, and as I've learned in my own homes, to fix or update a house is one thing. To restore it is yet another. A lot of times it takes twice the time and money to restore something to its former glory or at least its original time period. And if you want to use original materials—it's a real commitment. This is where design and lifestyle dovetail. You must really marry the idea of restoration—whether you do the work of restoration yourself or hire it out, to restore a space is a long and loving process. I remember in your first book, *Heart & Home,* there's a beautiful page I've turned to again and again where it says:

Purchasing a fixer upper in need of renovation and transformation can be the ultimate experience for the 'do it yourselfer.'.... This process requires an enormous amount of work, money and a certain amount of skill or willingness to learn the skills necessary to transform the mess before us.[2]

It certainly can turn some people off from DIY projects because they're all consuming. But I love that. And then you talk about how God desires to transform us using a beautiful verse from Romans: *And do not be conformed to this world, but be transformed by the renewing of your mind.*
Romans 12:2a NASB

God does desire to transform, which also reminds me of Psalms 51:12 *Restore to me the joy of your salvation and uphold me with a willing spirit.* It reminds me of restoration in my faith. We go through those periods where we are dried out or feel like we're in the desert, alone. I think it happens to everyone. But there are seasons where we just don't feel really joyful.

We may not feel energized; we don't feel useful. And God promises to restore to us the joy of our salvation—which is just beautiful. Just as you said, it's work and it doesn't happen overnight and it doesn't necessarily happen in our own strength, especially if we're talking about our soul. That's something that God does in us. And so being restored is just a beautiful thing. We get to be restored back to a new state!

---

2   page 141, *Heart & Home,* by Victoria Duerstock, 2019, Abingdon Press.

And I think about our souls, how do we neglect ourselves and find ourselves in a state where we need to be restored? What is it? Is it a quick process? Is it a slow slide? What do you see when you think about that?

I can certainly identify with the notion of needing to be restored. I think about the need to be restored every day it seems. As a mom in our contemporary world, I find it easy to become depleted and rest often feels impossible! In general, consumption of information and media sometimes can be depleting, and leaves a great longing to be restored. Our culture is quick to say, maybe a bath, a pedicure and a glass of wine can restore you. Unfortunately, in my case, that doesn't do it. In fact, those choices sometimes have other consequences that aren't that great. I've heard it said that our understanding of self-care in our present moment is the Band-Aid effect. Those things are fine on their own (for those who can handle them) but true restoration can only be found when we put ourselves in God's hands and ask to be restored as He would restore us.

> *He saved us, not because of works done by us in righteousness, but according to his own mercy, by the washing of regeneration and renewal of the Holy Spirit.*
>
> *Titus 3:5*

Sitting and being quiet are some of the most restorative things I can do. And sometimes they are the hardest things I know to do. But I can't replace quiet and solitude. That is

how God comes in and restores me. None of this comes easy
to me in any way as a compulsive doer or a "human doing" as
I've heard it said.

That's absolutely right, because if we're busy, we don't
have time to hear, and being still requires us to listen. And
sometimes I think we're just a little afraid to hear the things
that maybe we know we need to take care of in our lives. We
avoid being still because busyness feels better. It feels like
we're doing more.

This dovetails a little bit with the idea of prayer in our culture,
too. And this internal desire to do something. When people
are hurting or struggling, we feel like we need to be doing.
Yet our greatest offering that we can give people is praying
for them, being faithful to pray for needs. Unfortunately, we
tend to avoid prayer because it just doesn't seem to be as
much of an action as baking a cake or taking a meal, visiting,
or doing an errand, right? I don't know why we are kind of
wired that way. It just seems like the easy move is to go do
something, not sit and be still and pray.

Yes, I'm guilty of that—I love to bring people a meal. Not
because I'm a great cook but because it's action. But the
power is in the unseen, right? We must have faith in the
power of the unseen. And sometimes we're like my children,
who say, "I don't see God in this! Where is He?" We must
build the faith that tells us He's there always even when we
don't feel it. Prayer in and of itself is faith in the power of
something, even when we can't see or feel it, and even if the
people that are really hurting don't feel it and don't know of
or feel our prayers.

This wonderful pastor that I follow on Instagram, Pastor Ken Claytor, says, *God brings the super to our natural.* And I love that because I take my natural, my brokenness, my flaws and my weariness and I bring it to Him, and He adds the super. It *sure* doesn't mean I'm super, but it means that there's a supernatural experience that He uses for His glory, for His good, and for His plan. I'm not meant to bring the super. Conversely our culture says you can go and put your cape on and get it all done and knock it all out—maybe just double up on coffee. And sometimes restoring it all, getting it *all* done will give me such comfort. And look, I love my house clean. Really do. But sometimes I need to put myself to bed with a messy house, knowing I must be restored in a different way. And that's very humbling.

So true. The message of "you can do it all" is so bad for us. I mean, you can do it all, but not all today. We are just not meant to live these, like you said, supernatural lives, because that's not who we are. That's who God is. And we try to take that role from Him. I think that's when we find ourselves tired, wrung out and beat up at the end of the day or the end of the week or even the end of the year. And this year sure is putting us through the wringer anyway.

We are experiencing it in fast forward. I feel as if we're subjected to so many more things on an almost hourly basis. So being restored, especially now for me is just such a beautiful, beautiful word. There's a better future, there's a brighter tomorrow and there's hope. And I think that's where restoration brings me.

I love that and I believe we will be restored both in terms of our lives and with respect to who we are as a nation. But it's in God's time and it's in God's plan. We're not in control of that. And that's very humbling for us to not know the future. We don't know what anything is going to look like in the days ahead, but we have to trust that there will be restoration. I just keep saying, *Thy will, not mine be done.* Sometimes hourly! I've thought of having a big sign made with this actually! It's a lot about trusting the Lord has all of this.

Being restored is a process for all of us. Some seasons are harder than others, and yet we all experience them. Vulnerability links us together and helps us appreciate so much more the journey we are going through. Are you weary and tired of trying to do it all, all the time? We hope you are encouraged today to stop and recognize your need for restoration, and know that a pause, a deep breath, and rest may be the next step for your home and your heart.

Restore to me the joy of your salvation and
grant me a willing spirit, to sustain me.

—Psalm 51:12 NIV

RESTORING THE WOODEN PIECE THAT'S BEEN WAITING

a good hearty elbow grease project

You must have a piece of wooden furniture in your house that is old and worn and not in a charming way. We all have something like this. This piece doesn't necessarily need painting or to be reinvented. It just needs to have its material restored. Wood wears and ages poorly without being treated routinely. One of the simplest, easiest, most gratifying projects around the house is to **restore a piece of wood furniture with beeswax**. There are many furniture polish options but many have off-putting odors and chemicals or require multiple steps to apply. Not beeswax. My favorite brands are Daddy Vans and Touch of Oranges. Both restore wood pieces in just a few minutes, naturally. Both products are infused with essential oils, so they smell great too. You'll need a few old, dry rags, and about an hour, depending on the size of your project. This is a good step if you can't decide whether to refinish or paint. After a beeswax treatment, you should know the answer. There is also something satisfying about a simple elbow grease project. You'll have time to clear your mind, dig in, and then admire the fruits of your labor—after only 20-30 minutes depending on the size of your piece! The good feelings that come from elbow-grease projects have been documented by social scientists. They're good projects to do if you're feeling low about your house.

Chapter 4

REFURBISHED

refurbished: /ri-fer-bishd/ *adjective*

made to look new again by work such as painting, repairing, and cleaning[1]

When we refurbish, we often take stock of the parts of something—the parts of a piece of furniture, or a house. We also take stock of ourselves when we need God's healing hand on us. It's helpful to know God made us, from the tips of our toes to the hairs on our head. He knows all our parts. It's helpful in the home too, to know the parts we are working with. In the case of the home and the heart—it pays to look very closely. As we started digging a little deeper and preparing for this chapter, we looked at the definition closely. What does refurbish actually mean in this context? It's always interesting to find the layers of meaning in these definitions.

---

1 https://dictionary.cambridge.org/us/dictionary/english/refurbished

With my background as a musician, as a classically trained pianist specifically, I have some interesting memories and perspective to draw from as we look at these layers.

My very first piano was an antique that had to be restored rather than refurbished. The reason it had to be restored and not refurbished was because it had old strings, old hammers and more! We didn't want to replace any of the items inside of the cabinet, only restore them. This meant that the strings didn't get replaced and the hammers were still the originals. This was much more cost effective because my parents didn't want to invest a lot of money in this piano. Who knows if you're going to stick with it when you're eight years old!

This piano was wonderful, but the problem with having it refurbished was the strings were so old they could not be tuned to the note C, which everything is supposed to be tuned to. Doing that would have probably broken all the strings because of their age. So, the solution to this old string dilemma was to tune a half-step lower. I didn't really realize how much that affected me until I got to freshman music theory in college.

We did these ear training exercises. The professor would play several measures of music and we would listen for pitches and rhythms and then write them down on staff paper. And every single time I would be a half-step off! I never knew how much those years on that old piano had influenced me.

So, what is clear to me is that restoration keeps a lot of the original or replaces it with original materials, but a refurb needs new parts to give the object life again. I think that's the interesting nuance refurbished has; this idea of new materials being brought in, maybe even to give something a new purpose. Have you used refurbishing much with your items in your home?

Well, right now my mind's buzzing. I'm thinking about what my parents' 1980s house has done to my career. In all honesty, this is the first word I don't love—refurb isn't as elegant as restore. But now that I understand the distinction, I love the idea of using new materials versus trying to use what's there.
I love words and how none of them are quite the same.

The house we live in today is what I would call historically-irrelevant-1960s. It's not a colonial or craftsman, the two most-easily recognized or beloved American housing styles. It's not schoolhouse or Victorian, or a Cape Cod—it just is. But there are some unique trims and original details that have been hard to replicate. When we've renovated bathrooms, my contractor said, "We can have that original trim made, I think...but it's expensive and difficult." And he's a purist! So, I have said, "I'm not wedded to it, we're going to do something new." And so, I can say with confidence we've *refurbished* this house in lots of different ways as we've added and deleted doors, enlarged bathrooms and openings. We haven't done anything massive—just what I call "surgical strikes." And I have essentially invented new window/door/baseboard trim for all these projects—something I really like. I should say I really like trim and could go into a rabbit hole talking about it! All the woodwork, or millwork as it's also called, that surrounds doors and windows and runs along the baseboard tells you something about the house—often the age. And it also tells you if the house has been worked on. These details say a lot!

And when you do anything to the house you have this question—should we use all new materials—should we replace the hardware? Shall we invent a new trim? It's our choice to make in the creative journey that is house making: are you going to make it look like it did in its glory days or make it a wholly new creation which is so exciting?

Yeah, the whole new creation is kind of an interesting thought, too. In furniture markets recently, there were these interesting takes on some things that people crafted on their own in their backyards or workshops. There was this one bicycle table that was just awesome, and it really did well on Instagram. It was so funny.

People loved the picture that I took of it, but it was just a bicycle base, and someone had taken a big block of wood to place on top making a farmhouse style table. Now it's really cool because it's got a bicycle for a base and is just unique. Everybody that came through the showroom was turning and looking at the bicycle with a brand-new purpose.

It wasn't like you could ride that bicycle anymore. So, it gained a brand-new purpose as a table. I really like that part of the definition of refurbished as well has to do with purpose, because sometimes we struggle with purpose ourselves!

Yes, absolutely—what can we do with things that don't work for their original purpose? We have an obsession in our culture with new, new, everything new. I, however, think the idea of taking something old, and potentially discarded, and giving it new life in a new creation is fascinating.

There are so many artists that I've met on Instagram. They're using things, remaking them and refurbishing them for entirely new purposes. And I love the bike table, that's so fun. It's also becomes a work of art and a place where the family comes to eat, which is awesome.

Right, I mean, not everybody has a bicycle table. When you're creative, you put that creative touch on it. It just makes me think about the creative touch that God puts on our lives. He, as the creator, makes all things new. 2 Corinthians 5:17 tells us that if we are in Christ, we're *a new creation!*

We're not necessarily refurbed, He's actually making us brand new. We're not creating a new purpose or new look—we're being made brand new. And for me, that's an even greater purpose for us when we find this root of our faith in Christ.

To me that "taking root" means being open to what God's doing. That has been my spiritual challenge—to be open to how God wants to change, heal and use us, and what He has in store for us. Whether hearing His call or just being open to hearing His call can be very humbling. *I* want to be in charge. *I* want to drive the bus. *I* would be in charge of the refurb. But it's not always up to me. In fact, it's never up to me. I'm learning to be a willing participant. I am getting more and more used to this idea of God using us and making us new, even though we don't always get to choose. We might have a vision of who we'd like to become, who we'd like to serve, or how we'd like to serve but "Thy will not mine be done." Victoria, you have something you always say, that I often cling to—about the results being His. What is it?

Obedience is my job, and the results are His job.

I love that.

That's a great point. While you were talking, it made me think of how, when we're all functioning as we're supposed to in the church, there's great unity and beauty in the body.

But sometimes we want to be the eye, because we think that's going to be a more beautiful part of the body. And somebody else wants to be the hands. And sometimes we have ideas of what we should be doing for service to the kingdom or whatever. It becomes a lot about us instead of how we can bring glory to God. And when we are not obedient—when we don't lay down our pride or self or whatever is hindering us from being fully obedient—we hinder the beauty of the church functioning as it should. So, there's broader implications for me even as we're talking.

We are all the body of Christ! A refrain I've said over and over again this year, sometimes rocking in the corner, this crazy year! That means everybody—we don't exclude. Truly seeing our brothers and sisters as the body of Christ to me is a beautiful, open-hearted thing and it's not easy. There are times when my teenager is very fresh, and I'm not always able to see him as the body of Christ. When I'm getting shot with Nerf guns by my own people, keeping my heart open to where God has put me to serve can be hard. I do want to be the hands! But I am open Lord.

Absolutely, we would like to direct how our lives go. And the longer we live, I think the more we realize we can't. And yet that's the beauty. We can't see the overall picture either. We have our limited view and so we think we see more than what we do. And yet He is the one that has that all-encompassing view and puts us where He puts us. And what we have to do is just be obedient. Just do the job that we've been given to do and have a purpose. That bicycle may have wished to remain a bicycle. If it had a mind, it might have thought that was its purpose forever, right? Sometimes we think we're on a path to do something forever. And if we get offended or stuck on a shelf or left behind in some way, we may think there's nothing else out there for us. Yet there's always a purpose.

> By canceling the record of debt that stood against us with its legal demands. This he set aside, nailing it to the cross.
>
> Col. 2:14

I think there's never a trial without purpose, no suffering just for suffering's sake. I think there's always something beautiful that God can have come from it if we're willing. And sometimes a beautiful table comes out of a broken-down bicycle.

My friend Julie always says, "no suffering is ever wasted," and I've taken great comfort from those words. We can hang onto that especially in times of great trial or times when we may be tempted to wonder "why is this happening" throughout our day. This is very meaningful. I'm also glad you talked about this idea that God sees the overarching plan, but we can't.

Bringing it back to the home, this is a little counterculture,
for interior design.

We want to have a plan, deploy it and have everything fall in
place. Flip the switch, hang the art perfectly on the wall, and,
voila, everything is tied together just as it was on paper, just
like a TV show. That's certainly not how I operate, nor do
most people. Certainly planning is essential, and we always
start with a plan. We have a vision, but at the same time,
God is part of the process. We're subject to availability and
budget, and we give ourselves the freedom to step back and
say, "this hasn't worked the way I thought it would, now
that we're off paper." Clearly you can't "wait and see" with
everything—where are we going to put the water or gas line
must be planned out in the beginning of the process. But we
don't talk about that enough—about being open to how a
room takes shape over time. And in an urge to be "done" we
lose that flexibility. Let's put it this way, I strongly believe
God is part of any design project.

Well, He's the ultimate designer. I mean, He really is. And,
you know, all through the Bible, you can see examples of
his ultimate design. His fingerprints on the design of the
tabernacle, the design of the ark.[2] There are so many places
where there's just specific imprints of His order and His
design. And yet, you're right, we need to be flexible because
we just never know what any given day will bring. And we
don't know in our homes if we need a space for something else.

---

2   See the Book of Genesis 6, and Exodus 26, 27 et. al.

Sometimes plans change. Sometimes parents move in, sometimes parents move out. Sometimes we have to take care of others. And our homes are never static. They're always in a state of flux. We must be willing to adjust. And I think that's a beautiful thing that you brought up about design and being willing and accepting when changes come, because I'm not one that loves changes. I like for things to be set and this is how it's going to be. So, flexibility has always been hard for me. You know, my friends always go "pivot" and I'm like, oh no...

I do love change a little too much, you could say I'm a change addict! Which is not a great aspect of my personality—ask my husband! But what is good, I think, is allowing things to unfurl sometimes and not being so rigid in terms of my plan. It's hard! But God has come through on so many color choices or stressful furniture buys. Often I feel like the Lord has shown me something that was perfect that I didn't and wouldn't see until my own first seven choices failed!

Creativity and openness are required to think through refurbishing a home or piece of furniture. Whether we are DIYers or not—we need to see the possibilities with new parts or new life, in something old. The same is true of our hearts and souls: openness to God's miraculous work in us—trust in His love for us—will help us to become the people He desires us to be in this life. Is God encouraging you to let something go, for more peace, calm and consolation? If so, can you pray for the willingness to let go?

Therefore if any man be in Christ, he is a new creature: old things are passed away; behold, all things are become new.

—2 Corinthians 5:17 KJV

For thus says the One who is high and lifted up, who inhabits eternity, whose name is Holy: "I dwell in the high and holy place, and also with him who is of a contrite and lowly spirit, to revive the spirit of the lowly, and to revive the heart of the contrite."

Isaiah 57:15

Chapter 5

RECLAIMED

reclaimed: /ri-klam-d/ *adjective*

describing something that's been recalled from wrong or im-
proper conduct or rescued from an undesirable state, also:
restored to a previous natural state[1]

Reclaimed is a word that's equally powerful, useful and full
of imagery both in the design world and in the spiritual realm.
We have a deep desire to reclaim things when we see value—our
creativity is on fire when we reclaim something. It feels so good!
And, God, our Creator has reclaimed us, Hallelujah!

I can tell this topic is just so full for us. This is a good one!
Starting with that definition...*to reclaim is to rescue from
an undesirable state or to regain possession,* it has so many
meanings. But I'm going to throw it back to you, Victoria,
because I know how much you love this word! I have seen
in *Heart and Home* so many beautiful examples of reclaimed

---

1 www.mirriam-webster.com/dictionary/reclaim

items and using history in the home. I'm guessing this word might be your favorite!

It really has become my favorite! Some of the features we photographed for *Heart and Home: Design Basics for Your Soul & Living Space* came from my friend's home. She has this lovely place with these beautiful pieces that have come from all kinds of places. There are wood beams that were from Abraham Lincoln's era, and there are banisters for her stairs that are from New York City stoops. I mean, these pieces have stories.

And I was just so enamored. The home is beautiful. So, you don't even necessarily know the story when you see all the pieces, you just see a beautiful home. But then she begins telling you where the different things come from, and it's exciting. She shares story after story of items that are not just pieces that came from a random furniture store. Every piece of furniture, every accessory and even the flooring have stories. And I just love that, because that story lives on.

Oh, my gosh. Well, first of all, you had me at "banister from New York City stoops." That's incredible because we think of reclaimed items maybe in terms of furniture or flooring. Reclaimed barn wood, as you've mentioned, is something that's become so popular and for good reason. Adding architectural elements made of stone from elsewhere into the structure of the home is just so unique and interesting – that's next level!

There's a basic human desire to be around pieces of history and things that have had a former life. This is why we love thrift stores—or at least, some of us! Whether it's china from another other woman's home or these big architectural elements, old is entrancing. Any kind of salvage but especially *architectural salvage* is my jam. When a home is demolished and all the architectural "parts" of the home are destroyed (windows, doors, trim, cornices, etc.), it's a shame, especially for older homes. But getting to reclaim and rescue these pieces is an incredible opportunity—as well as a very romantic idea.

Even the strictest minimalist would find something incredibly special about taking something from another era into their space. I have seen "relics" from the early space age, George Jetson-like objects (think Sputnik) that are popular in more contemporary spaces. Nobody can deny the romance in using a piece of history—I'll make that claim.

I like how you have staked your flag on this one! I even think about brick from old buildings being reclaimed and used for new builds, and even wood from the Saratoga Stables. We were at a furniture market within the last few years and the showroom was full of beautiful lighting and light fixtures. Many of them had these unique wood accents or beams reclaimed from the stables in Saratoga, New York.

These were the actual boards from the stables where the horses stayed when they raced. But this barn's run down and not being used anymore. It needs to be rescued. And somebody had this brilliant idea to use those pieces of wood to create something new. Each lamp even came with its own written history—its own story. You could read about it. It was so meaningful for me because I love words and I love story. Unfortunately, that meant I wanted everything in the showroom! Ha!

I love it. The authenticity is what makes that truly special—that it really was from where it said it was from. And people might think, "well, that's really expensive and it's hard to come by." Yes, perhaps an authenticated fixture from a Saratoga racing stable might be beyond your budget. But this idea can work on many different levels. When we moved into this house, there was an original brass lighting fixture on the porch ceiling that didn't work for us. I took it down, dumped maybe 200 dead insects out, and saw how truly unique it was in my hand. It had to have a second life in the house, somehow.

I thought *I cannot throw this away.* I mean, it doesn't take much for me as I've been called a packrat, but I'm a sentimental packrat! I took some Brasso to this fixture and it's now a hurricane lamp with a candle and I love it. Even though I've replaced the fixture, it now lives on in a different way. This notion is not just meant for people that can buy authentic antiques—I think this idea is really for all of us.

That's true. As we think about space in the home, we've talked a little bit about this before, it's so important to consider how we use space and practice flexibility. But how do we reclaim space in our home?

You know, I think sometimes we have to say to ourselves, no, this space is not working in this structure as is. This happened to me. I needed to shift from what I was comfortable with "pre-Covid" because everybody was working outside of the home. I had the space here to myself. And then everybody came home to stay, and they would want to go to the refrigerator right when I'd be trying to record.

This made me frustrated and unhappy. I had been comfortable in my routine and my quiet space and now I was having to reconsider all of it. I eventually needed to reclaim space in the home where I could do my work. How does that apply with you as well—having to reclaim space sometimes? Do you have to work at that?

Yes, certainly. As women and moms, that's hard for us. We give everything, right? We're giving right, left and center—to the family, to an employer, to someone in the community who may need us—sometimes all at once! And sometimes this leads to a breakdown. We need to reclaim a space for ourselves, and a way to make ourselves more useful and less pulled apart. As you and I have discussed many times, I have often tried to work among and amidst my children—with everyone home. While they worked. While they played. While we have attempted "online school." And it's been a failure. You were the one to suggest that although I had to adjust a few things with how I worked, finding quiet and a place to focus was really

> *"For I will restore health to you, and your wounds I will heal," declares the Lord, "because they have called you an outcast: 'It is Zion, for whom no one cares!'"*
>
> *Jeremiah 30:17*

necessary. I am now reclaiming a portion of my bedroom because I need to have a place where I am alone to work best. I didn't see it until my original plan failed.

You helped me see this idea—that I have to reclaim space where I can be quiet because God's reclaimed me! As you know, I believe for much of my early life I was wandering in the desert, or God only knows where, looking for Him "in all the wrong places." And now I feel so reclaimed by the Lord. I need to have a place to intentionally go back to Him—each and every day.

All this to say, my reclaimed space will be where I read scripture or sketch out a new cabinet for somebody. It'll be the same spot. And I need it to be a place with a door nearby!

A door is so handy.

And with locks. Quite necessary!

This reminds me of the verse in 1 Timothy, about why Messiah came. "It is a trustworthy saying that deserves complete acceptance to this world, Messiah came sinful people to reclaim." Isn't it beautiful to see our word reclaim there? God is claiming us again and rescuing us. And He is the ultimate rescuer. What a beautiful word picture one more time in the Bible!

First of all, I look forward to someday having your grasp of scripture or even half of your grasp of scripture. But, wow, that verse speaks to my heart! In my years of dysfunction,

I wasn't looking for Christ at all, wasn't looking, wasn't interested. And He still pursued me.

And I always say this: if He pursued me, He's pursuing everybody, because I was neither looking nor interested. I even had a lot of disdain for organized religion. I wasn't sure if I was a Christian. And I feel reclaimed over many, many years. It wasn't like there was a burning bush. There were, however, decades of smoking embers in the corner. And, in really responding to that, I really feel very much rescued. Absolutely. I mean, that analogy works very well for me in my story.

I guess that's why I love the word reclaimed so much because it's about the story! A story that we tell means something to someone else. Your story is unique to you. When we share our stories, we get to say how good God is because He met us where we were! We have no idea what our story can do for somebody else. I think it's vastly important we share our stories and, beyond that, the beauty of being reclaimed by God.

This reminds me of this expression, "I didn't wake up like this." What I say is "I wasn't born like this." Or maybe I was born like this, but I made a mess of things before arriving here. The reclaiming process took a long time. And I think sometimes when I look at myself now and where I am in my prayer life, I think "oh dear, so far yet to go."

But I know a little scripture, and I'm going to God every chance I get. I'm now even reclaiming myself for God—how I use my energies and parts of my day. Who we become is truly in God's time: He has His hands in our process, our story. There's something I heard today, "As your story is unfolding, remember, you're not the editor." I thought that was good.

Yes. And that's good because I'm not the best editor. I miss a lot of stuff. I make mistakes.

My least favorite part of writing is the editing!

I need a good editor, absolutely. Now, I think being reclaimed is beautiful. And I think it's a beautiful thing for us to consider in our homes and anywhere that we can put something that's reclaimed.

My friend loves to surround herself with beautiful things that have been reclaimed, and that have a story. This is partly because her story has to do with being adopted and not knowing significant parts of her family history. That just touches my heart in much the same way our homes and the assembled items in them bring us connection. They hold reminders, if you will, of what grandma's house was like or reminders of a past age. Reminders are always so good because they help us stay focused, stay centered and fill us with joy.

You've opened up a whole new pathway, Victoria, on this topic! Reclaiming has this other dimension—that the home doesn't have to be what people have told you it needs to be. You can actually reclaim what "home" means. This is healing for those who have childhood wounds or anyone who just wants to re-establish what the home will be for themselves.

Home certainly doesn't have to be exactly what we see in the marketplace or what we're told on Instagram or whatever. This is part of the creative process, creating a space that is beautiful, yes, but also honors what we need. And that sometimes requires us to break rules. I often go with what works for me, whether other people are doing it or not. I ask my clients as well—does it work for you? It's ok that everyone else is doing something different—in fact, in my case I like that a little better.

Lately, it's been essential to reclaim our day from the clutches of busyness, family craziness or bad news on TV. That's another way we must reclaim, Victoria, we're barely scratching the surface here on this awesome word!

To reclaim is to use a certain creative power, it's a way of seeing things in different ways—and then bringing something somewhere else—harnessing the power of history, or storytelling. Reclaimed barnwood does more than just keep wood from the landfill, we bring the essence of the barn, of another place from another time and perhaps another way of living, into our lives which may be quite far from rural life. When we think about what Jesus went through and how He came to us—to reclaim us—it's startling but should also make us feel profoundly loved and adored. What can you reclaim for yourself, to bring you closer to God?

It is a trustworthy saying that deserves complete acceptance to this world, Messiah came sinful people to reclaim.

—1 Timothy 1:15 ISV

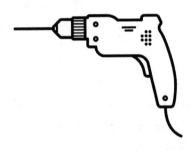

BE THE LIGHT

an easy, inexpensive way

Lighting is so important in a home—it helps us to extend our day beyond sundown and can make us feel energized or relaxed. It helps us do things—complete tasks in the kitchen, read to a child, warm up a dining room when just candlelight isn't enough to see what's on the plate. One of my favorite lighting "tricks" is the use of plug-in wall sconces. This is a trick because, when you add a light source to a space, usually you need to open up walls and hire an electrician. With a plug-in, you don't. You just plug the fixture in and secure it to the wall with screws. No electrical work! There is a cord, but this can be channeled and then painted to match the wall. Or you can get an interesting cord and live with it as it is. Plug-ins, because of the cord, are best above a piece of furniture such as a console, night table or dresser. They are a great way of "inserting" light for softness or reading or just to bring the lighting down a bit. Builders love recessed lights, but they can be dominant—and a little boring even on dimmers. Wall sconces add unique shapes in light and they're not that expensive! Check Overstock.com, or Wayfair.com and search for "plug-in wall sconces."

Chapter 6

RENEWED

renewed[1]/ri-nud/

1: made like new; restored with freshness, vigor or perfection

2: regenerated

3: restored into existence

Renewal means a fresh start. Just like spring, we sense a shift and know that things are going to be made new again and restored. Whether it's the exterior of our home that needs a good pressure washing or an interior declutter and clean, being renewed doesn't necessarily require a massive monetary investment but certainly requires a shift in perspective! And small renewing steps lead to bigger ones.

Victoria, who doesn't want renewal right now? Whether it's a change to the house or a new year when the old one felt hard—we all love the chance for *brand new*. And with our

---

1 http:www.merriam-webster.com/dictionary/renew

conversation here I think we can offer some encouragement and perhaps a new perspective on renewal. Look, for better or worse, social media and the things we see online or in print set up an expectation of perfection with the unlived-in glossiness of the perfect home. That can feel overwhelming, taunting us with impossible standards disconnected to how people really live. We may start to think: if I don't have a huge budget or if I don't have a huge home or if I don't live on a cliff overlooking the water, then what I have isn't good enough, or worse yet, "my life isn't good enough.".

And I wish people knew that renewal doesn't have to be the beautiful new house on a cliff in Malibu. Renewal can happen in profoundly simple ways. One of our purposes for this book is to breathe new life into words like renewal for the home—it isn't always a ton of work or radical change.

Sometimes a fresh perspective on the home comes from simply tidying up the room. I have found, for myself, taking small steps leads to greater ideas and solutions for the bigger stuff. But if my house is a mess and I feel a lot of despair about my environment, or too much "stuff," I have zero chance of renewal—big or small.

Renewal can be even just the simple things—the deep clean or a pressure washing for the outdoors. There's just something about a fresh house that feels like things are good again.

It's so much fun to see how this kind of work breathes new life into that space. I'm even thinking about the backdrop behind me. These brass floral panels have been in almost every room of our house. I mean, they migrate, you know, so they're not "fixed" fixtures. But every time they come into a new space, it's like a renewal.

I love that you brought those panels up—I need a yin to your yang with my plain white doors here behind me—I need something to work on! Send me a set or perhaps I'll spray paint mine! Pink? Too many projects over here! But seriously what I hear you talking about is "shopping" your home. In our culture, we're taught to buy, buy, buy our way out of any kind of discomfort. But we can use, re-use, reposition, move around, replace almost everything in our home, especially when we have a need for change all the time as I do!

Renewal all too often means buying new things. This leads to a false renewal in my opinion. And I don't count paint as a purchase by the way. This is because to me paint is graduate-level cleaning. Paint, like a good clean, just does justice to what we already have. But in terms of filling your house with new stuff, what can I say? New things can be wonderful. I don't begrudge anybody buying new things, and I have been known to indulge in retail therapy. Yet it doesn't make a great house. It may only salvage a moody afternoon.

> *Then he said to the man, "Stretch out your hand." And the man stretched it out, and it was restored, healthy like the other.*
>
> *Matthew 12:13*

One great way to begin the process of renewal is to empty your space entirely. Give yourself the gift of a blank slate. Just the process is so renewing; to be able to clean everything out. A few years ago, a friend, who is also an organizer, came to my house to help me deal with "the piles" as I had recently helped her choose some furnishings for her living room. I had papers piled up waist high. I had four kids that were all in different stages of pre- and primary school and each day they brought more paper home. I didn't know what to do with all this paper, so every day the pile got worse. I'm very nostalgic and I kept almost everything. She said to me, "OK., We're going to throw out what's easy to throw out, and then put the rest into boxes and put it in the attic. If you have to keep it, you can't keep it in here anymore. And you're going to set a date and organize it later." What I didn't realize is that I couldn't even think straight until that pile was gone. Although it is not gone, but it is "away." I know someday I'll go through and decide which papers are to be kept for my son's wives or whatever. My friend also gave me a new way of dealing with incoming paper—which was to keep very, very little!

The point is, I had renewed my room in one day. It was empty. Now, was everything solved? No, but I gave myself a gift of the blank space then and tackling those boxes when I am ready will be doable. The renewal wasn't about organizing or purging everything, (i.e., becoming a different person) in order to redo the whole room. It was simply giving myself that open space, which is where this desk now sits.

Yeah, I think that's important. Sometimes we have to remove the things that weigh us down. It's interesting because this idea fits perfectly with the verses for our renewal theme.

2 Corinthians 4:16-18 *Therefore, we do not lose heart, though outwardly we are wasting away. Yet inwardly we are being renewed day by day for our light and momentary troubles are achieving for us an eternal glory that far outweighs them all. So, we fix our eyes not on what is seen, but what is unseen since what is seen is temporary, but what is unseen is eternal.* That renewal that's happening inside of us every day is not something we're at work doing, but something that God is doing in us though we are wasting away on the outside. Unfortunately, we're aging, you know. I so feel that deep in my heart. But we are being renewed daily.

We can be refreshed. We can wake up in the morning with a blank slate. That's one of my favorite things to think about, is that every day is new. It's like a fresh piece of paper that hasn't seen any marks on it. And every day we're being renewed and that's just the same way it is inside of our hearts and our souls.

I love it. I mean, that's also very 12-Step-y, where I learned (in AA) that every day is new one day, and we get there one moment at a time. Even the Lord's Prayer, which I first heard in an AA meeting in a church basement, says, "give us this day our daily bread." We just get one day to make with it what God and I can do together. I love that. For some of us that might be on the moodier side. We can get down in the dumps about our work or health or relationships.

And we may think, "where do I begin?" We must remember: God is working alongside us, but sometimes those renewals happen in small, even tiny, stages every new day. Just like you're not going to redo your home in a day or even a whole room despite what they show on TV (what a lie, by the way), God works on us bit by bit, poco a poco, as they say in Spanish.

Calling TV projects a lie isn't totally fair. What I mean is there is a month's work that is edited down to twenty-two minutes of airtime. In reality, even an hour project of mine takes a lot of planning and thought—as much as a week's worth! And like the bedroom that I'm sitting in right now, clearing that space was the only way to even get to a place where I could address what else I wanted to do. Life really does work in bite-sized chunks.

As you've mentioned it's consumerism that plagues us in general and imparts this feeling that we need more stuff. The reality is, most of us have too much stuff and perhaps what we need to do is rotate the things we do have every so often. You can pull it out of that room and put it away for a little while.

Maybe you still love it. You don't want to get rid of it yet. That's fine. But you don't need to have all the stuff out in all the places all the time. That's where clutter becomes a problem. As you said earlier, if you can't think you can't function. You can't. We tend to get in a mood and dwell on our feelings and then we're not good for anything.

So, it's not good in our homes to have too many things. Yet that's the idea behind "retail therapy." Right? That's just how we're supposed to operate if we listen to everyone else.

It is, and I think we don't talk enough about what we want to express, which isn't always achieved through buying. But as you did with your panels, you can shop your home. You can also delete and take away. And when you have that itch to create a vignette or something beautiful, perhaps to reflect the seasons, we have many choices.

In summertime, social media is already talking about fall, maybe even Christmas. Frankly, I sometimes wouldn't mind Christmas in October based on how the year is going, but people are always a little too ready for the next season on Instagram. You don't have to run to a store and buy what's coming next. Seasonality is about what's going on outside and bringing it inside. The seasons really are just what trees are doing—budding, flowering, losing leaves, etc. Some seasons lend themselves to less (such as summer) and we can give ourselves permission to have seasons without any decor at all!

I don't know—if we're going to the store and we're buying new stuff with the intention of making ourselves feel better, that's not the best place from which to create a home. That's not a great foundation. And by the way, if we've got discomfort and issues, there might be a better way to deal with them than Target.

I agree. I mean, we go shopping because it makes us feel better. But really does it? You know, when I get the credit card bill or have that argument with my husband over our budget and finances, ten times out of ten I don't feel better at all. And so, are we really helping ourselves? Or should we be learning to be content with the space and things that we do have and freshening them up instead?

As you said, there's nothing wrong with paint, a deep clean or removing the clutter. Those are the things we can do without investing a ton of money. And many, many times those things make us feel good—there's nothing like a good, deep clean. And that sense of satisfaction when you're done and you're thinking that spot on the counter looks *good*.

My house might not all look good, but that spot looks good!

Yes, during the quarantine there was a lot of cleaning going on nonstop, you know? I needed my space as clean & fresh as I ever have. And again, that's that need for renewal. It happens every day because kids need to eat every minute of every day it seems.

That's right. I feel like I have just fed them and they're asking again, what's for the next meal? And I'm like, I just cooked. And then I just got it all cleaned up.

So now I get to do it again, you know.

How could it be all gone? But it is.

They're growing.

Yeah, they are.

I mean I eat too. So, you know.

> Oh yes, me too, and not like a bird! And I'm also making a
> mess. So, I am tidying up after myself too!

The whole idea of renewal should be so encouraging. I mean, it's just a beautiful thing to think of being renewed day by day, of renewing our spaces with what we have already without a need to go get something else. It's nice in those moments when we have a need, and we can do something. But it's also an opportunity to think through what we already have and how we could reuse it.

I think you do that well. You love to move things around and place them in different spots and play with that. My kids have gotten that bug. They flip their bedrooms all the time. I'm always walking into a bedroom, smacking into a bed, and thinking, well, that wasn't there before, but now it is! They all do it and they love it. It's just freedom giving you an opportunity to arrange the space in a different way and see it in a new light.

> I'm never going to get rid of that itch that says I want to
> change something. But it doesn't always mean buying
> something new. Sometimes it means we move something
> around—your kids are after my own heart!

Renewal doesn't have to be an investment of money in your home. As a matter of fact, we would argue that it's just the opposite. Being renewed can simply be removing the clutter and cleaning it up. Next time you think, "I need a new...." can you pause and ponder if you can answer the need in a creative way with what you already have? Our hearts and homes benefit when we pursue renewal in this way!

Therefore we do not lose heart. Though outwardly we are wasting away, yet inwardly we are being renewed day by day. For our light and momentary troubles are achieving for us an eternal glory that far outweighs them all. So we fix our eyes not on what is seen, but on what is unseen, since what is seen is temporary, but what is unseen is eternal.

—2 Corinthians 4:16-18 NIV

A Psalm of David. The Lord is my shepherd; I shall not want. He makes me lie down in green pastures. He leads me beside still waters. He restores my soul. He leads me in paths of righteousness for his name's sake. Even though I walk through the valley of the shadow of death, I will fear no evil, for you are with me; your rod and your staff, they comfort me. You prepare a table before me in the presence of my enemies; you anoint my head with oil; my cup overflows.

Psalm 23:1-6

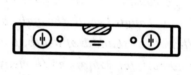

Chapter 7

REFOCUSED

refocused[1]: re/fo/kes *adjective*

1: to have found focus again

2: to have changed the emphasis or direction of

The opportunity to refocus is the opportunity to pivot. When we lose our focus, we have a chance to decide once again what it is that we really want to focus on. Distractions keep us from keeping an eye on our focal point! This is as true in the spiritual realm as it is in the material world. Being intentional with our focus helps us to thrive in this life rather than just survive.

We are having these conversations in 2020, so if you ever come across these in the year 2030, just understand what was happening back then. In these days the lack of focus that we're all experiencing is the result of having no idea how much "stuff" is coming at us on any given day, whether it's

---

1 Refocus | Definition of Refocus by Merriam-Webster (merriam-webster.com)

trials in the world, or trials here at home such as getting kids back in school. All this stuff is happening all the time.

And in these moments focus is super hard in our home, or even in our design. I know you can talk about that. That's important in a room.

Well, it is, it's funny, the focal point has been piles of laundry in my house! As you mentioned, many people have young children or grown children more or less "stuck" at home and there's really no end in sight to all the time *at home*. (Even when the lockdowns ended, schools and businesses remained closed.) And as a result, there's a lot of chaos in the home for everyone I've spoken to. It's hard to get beyond just the day to day of cleaning and tidying and so forth—getting beyond those laundry mountains.

But, yes, if we can get there, every space needs a focal point. Our eyes naturally want to choose something to focus on. When you walk into a room; your eyes are naturally drawn to something. And in design we hope to direct that in a specific way. Sometimes I'll walk into different rooms and say to myself, "What do I see first? Wait a second, is it an outlet or the thermostat? Is that piece of art crooked?" This can be a challenge for the OCD among us because we can hyper-focus on those little things! But it's a good exercise!

In my bedroom, I have a gallery wall that I want to look at—because it's full of art I love—it's there for a reason, and my eyes are attracted to it. It's the way our bodies work; to be drawn in by things we love because of their placement and how we feel about them. And we get to be intentional about it. If we're not intentional, we're automatically drawn to the things that say, "look at me!" whether we want to or not. We can say, "I want the focal point to be this beautiful piece of art, that makes me feel so good." It reminds me of this great trip I took with my husband. Or I want the focal point to be this beautiful collection on the mantel. In that case we need to "quiet down" everything else. But we do want a focal point and it's going to happen anyway. So, the more intentional we can be, the better.

I love that you pointed out that it's an intentional choice that we make to have a focal point in a room, whether that's a mirror or a wall or a piece of art. When we're intentional, we can then design around it. It's the point and everything else happens around it. I think that's the same thing I find in my heart, in my soul, when I am out of focus, disjointed and all wrong, I realize that my focus has been taken off where it's supposed to be.

You know Hebrews 12:1 talks about this. It is another one of my favorites. And we literally just finished talking about how much this whole chapter means to both of us. I'm going to read the first two verses because it really does talk about where our focus is supposed to be in our hearts.

Therefore, since we are surrounded by so great a cloud of witnesses, let us lay aside every weight and sin which clings so closely and let us run with endurance, the race that is set before us, looking to Jesus, the founder and protector of our faith, who, for the joy that was set before Him, endured the cross despising the shame and is seated at the right hand of the throne of God.

There's so much!

> I have chills, Victoria, because we did not discuss this beforehand but that very verse has gotten me through this quarantine and this year. I have it on post-it notes, and postcards & I carry it with me. There's something about clearing out the sinfulness, and whatever is in us that's in our way, so that we may persevere with a cloud of witnesses. Not joking, I've got goosebumps. That verse has really been a real source of strength.

Yeah, absolutely, because I like how those two verses are packed with such good truth. Right? Like the Christian walk, our faith journey is not a sprint. It's definitely a marathon. It demands endurance *and* perseverance. It's a race. But also, when we keep our eyes on the right spot, we're going to end up in the right place. That can't happen if we become unfocused and take our eyes off Jesus, the One doing the work in us.

And He is the One that's already done it. And all we need do is rely on it and trust in obedience. But when we get focused on what's happening here or why I'm unhappy or the world around me, chaos, confusion, murder hornets, whatever, I'm not focused where I'm supposed to be. And I can't live my life with joy, with faith, with substance.

I'm too distracted. Removing those distractions is so important. I think it's the same in our homes. We've talked about this already, I know. But decluttering and removing the extra stuff is sometimes half the battle.

It is! So often when people hire me and I walk into their home, I'm able to see the potential for a great focal point, that they can't see. I might walk in and say, "oh, my gosh, look at this beautiful thing that you have! We just need to kind of move stuff out of the way you can so you can see it!" Or "We need to hang it higher or lower." Sometimes people will have a lovely piece of furniture and they have put it in a place where they can't even enjoy it.

Sometimes we just need to shift focus. Sometimes I'm just the fresh eyes. We're not talking about ordering something new that only I can find, or a custom-made piece. We're talking about fresh eyes for what people already have. And I think that's what holy friendship does. It's a gift to have friends who guide us on our way and help us refocus. I'm so grateful to be able to say that I finally have, in my life, women in whom I trust and can confide, who guide me, and encourage me. They can be counted upon to tell me the truth and give me fresh eyes on a problem or relationship.

> *Restore us, O Lord God of hosts! Let your face shine, that we may be saved!*
>
> *Psalm 80:19*

And when I hear that verse from Hebrews, what I get is this: yes, there were murder hornets and incredible divisiveness in today's world, but I still have to wake up in the morning and deal with my own sinfulness. It's not going to go away just like that and certainly not by hyper-focusing on problems of the world. You could even say my sinfulness is magnified and drawn out when I hyper-focus on the problems of the world. As they say, "you can either get bitter or you can get better." I don't get better merely by waking up in the morning—it takes real work.

I love that. We do the work, and we allow God to bring the results. I mean, it's that same conversation we've already had. But we need the reminder! We forget and we want to handle the results. We feel results are up to us when it's actually a matter of us just doing the work that we know we're supposed to do. Our part is to stay connected to the work and run the race with patience, endurance, perseverance, and faith.

We must be faithful in our homes to stay focused. It's intentional. And I bring it back to where you started: an intentional choice. When my household feels out of sync and out of whack, I must intentionally sit down and say, "OK, what's going on? What do we have to do to fix this?" When everybody's schedules are wild and you're going in a thousand directions at once, sometimes you need to pull back, right?

You have to sit down and say, OK, the limit is one activity per week or one per child (which is still a lot when you've got more than more than one). Ultimately you have to reassess and be intentional with your time and where you're spending it. This is still true. Even in the middle of the last year it was more true. But you know, the intentionality of being in God's word every day, of being in prayer every day, that's huge too, because if that's not my focus, it's super easy to let that slide. Right?

The typical excuse has been I don't have time to really dig in and read my Bible or I don't have time to pray. And if there's anything that the pandemic and quarantine taught us is this: we've got time. Our excuse that we don't have the time is invalid. Rather, we lack intention. It's at the end of the day where are our true intentions are to be found.

Well, and there's lots of distractions, right? Like this phone right next to me—huge culprit. I think that's our job really, even as a parent, to help our kids manage the distractions in their lives. We make sure they get outside and be kids. Intentionally I can do what's best for me also and focus on the main thing for mind, body and soul every single day.

But I have to manage the many distractions. I think even that's true in the home. We must constantly revisit what's in the home, and if it rings true. When you walk in the home and encounter a huge bucket of helmets and sports paraphernalia, it's time to move it elsewhere if those sports aren't happening for your kids right now. Unless you live in a part of the country where sports are resuming, you probably don't need that bucket at all, or you just need to address it season to season. We need to constantly look at the home, walk around, and ask, "what do we need for the time we're in?"

I just think being honest about where we are in this exact moment is necessary and having a baby illustrates this point very well. You'll go through these stages where you need all this stuff, but obviously it's not forever. So, we constantly retool. Do I still need the walker, or do I still need bassinet? Do I still need that? Do we still need the monitor? And that phase really trained me in a way to constantly evaluate the house: is this still set up for our life?

I'm highly focused on aesthetics. I want things to look and feel beautiful, but they really don't feel beautiful when they don't work. Look for things that serve no purpose or fail to meet the family's needs. Maybe there's no bin for the masks that need to be laundered or there's no place for keys or helmets for the football player—think about function.

We're often focused on the spread from Pottery Barn or how we want something to look, not considering what our day-to-day functions require. I think it needs to begin there.

Yes! It's true because our lives are seasonal, right? What is true for us right now in this season doesn't mean our lives will always look like this. Yet we need to optimize and be intentional about how things look today and let our homes serve us well in this moment.

I saw this great spread recently. I was looking through *ELLE Decor*, which is gorgeous.

Right? It's one of those magazines you look at and you're inspired. You think, that's great for other people. I mean, you know, it would be great.

Exactly, and in this particular magazine I loved this one extremely cool layout for a family with a very modern aesthetic. They went with very modern surfaces, very minimal. Yet in the big spread of the kitchen, they actually included pictures with Lucky Charms and a pitcher of milk on the table. I

thought kudos to them because they were not cleaning it out
to make the kitchen look unlived in. Another thing shown
was this ginormous centerpiece made of an upside-down
dum-dum lollipop that had melted across the table.

I just loved it. I mean - how fun for kid? Like, you could tell they
had children in the family. And they love a modern aesthetic.
They loved the look. They made sure to incorporate it for
their family at the same time. And I was just so impressed.
I was just super impressed with that spread because it spoke
to me that we're making room for the people that live in our
home, making it fun, accessible and intentional.

Perhaps in 15 years when the kids move out, they're not
going to have a big dum-dum lollipop in the middle of the
table as the featured centerpiece. But it's fun for right now
and it's great for the family.

I love that and I love the playfulness. The idea that we have to
grow up and be really sophisticated in our home is just silly.
Try to be sophisticated with little children—it's impossible.

To be playful in your home is a gift. Kids ask for that. We
need to think, where are we and what season are we in? Are
we evolving with the kids or asking them to live in a super-
sophisticated space which only disappoints them because
they don't understand why they can't play or be themselves
in these spaces? I'm certainly experiencing that in my kids
now, who have a lot of opinions about the house and the
way they want it to be. I'm glad they're engaged. Shocking,
I know, considering I have four very opinionated people
living with me.

I think it's funny because you're right. When they're little, you're just happy to be fully clothed when you leave the house and not have spit-up all over you. We've lived those years, you know, where our shirts have permanent stains. And we ask, will life ever look differently?

The answer is yes, it does. It does. It's a season. Then you go to the next season, you ask, will this ever end? And yeah, it will. It always does. Along the way they become opinionated young people, which has its own fun and drama. But it's fun to watch the seasons. When we're flexible in those seasons, I think we have more fun in our home, more fun with the people who mean the most to us, the ones we love the most.

And our spaces can reflect that, too.

So, I have a question for you in that scripture that we read from Hebrews, which I love. I'm a scripture novice but I want to know more, specifically about this verse. I'm not sure who the "cloud of witnesses" is. Sometimes, as I read that I think of the cloud of witnesses as being my children. I am home with my kids a lot, as are many others. Surrounded by them you might say. Surrounded by people looking to me, all the time.

I want to meet their needs and I want the house to reflect their personalities. Also, the kids are a reminder to refocus on what's important. Sometimes I don't have an inherent desire to get on my knees or open my Bible. Nevertheless, my children, as my witnesses, are the "eyes on me." Maybe that's not the appropriate use of that scripture though that's what comes to mind. I'm reminded, "there are people watching, what are you focused on?" Am I deep-diving into online shopping for stuff I don't need or staring at my phone? Or am I reading the scripture of the day every day or do I routinely pray? They really are my motivation. I would love to know your take on that.

Well, I love that because it's true. The people around us and with us, especially our families, don't always get the best of us, right? They sometimes get the most comfortable of us, which is not always our best. We save that usually for strangers, which really should not be. But it is the reality of our lives.

They are watching and we do want to set a good example. We want to lead them to not just do as I say but do what I do as well. As a mom, that's something that I take to heart constantly; how well am I leading? Am I training them well? And if not, I need to reassess and refocus quickly because that's not what I want.

You know, often you're looking at verses in scripture in order to really know the meaning. I love it when pastors say if there is a "therefore" in your verse, you want to look at what it's "there for." And the reason that word is there is because at the end of Hebrews 11, known as the Hall of Faith chapter in my understanding, it talks about all the people that have given their lives or people from the Old Testament that lived lives of faith, who even though they didn't have sight of what was coming, believed God would supply all their needs.

The end of Chapter 11 is about martyrs, people who died for their faith, people who didn't get to see the promise in this life, and yet they lived by faith. They didn't get to see how God was going to provide. Because of their witness, because of their lives, we are surrounded by that knowledge, that information. Because they were worthy to live their lives in such a way we can as well. I think that's encouraging to listen to these people of great faith in Chapter 11. Look at what they did, how they lived their lives, even if they didn't get to see.

Therefore, since we're surrounded by this information, we should also live in such a way. For me, that's the real bottom line. And I do love your practical application of needing to make sure my children see me living out this faith so that I also can be a person of faith.

I appreciate that and I've got to go read Chapter 11!

It's so good. Hebrews 11 is a great reminder of all the people that have lived worthy; they weren't perfect. I think that that's encouraging too. We're not perfect. We're just being called, despite ourselves, to keep our eyes focused on what we've been promised, what God's word teaches us, and knowing that He is the finisher of this faith.

Well, if anyone who is reading has not noticed, Victoria knows her scripture, and I don't. I'm new to it, but I'm new to it in a way that I feel that it hits me hard. I don't know if that makes any sense or maybe it's because I waited so long. I don't know.

Well, I mean, we both travelled different paths too and I think that that's what makes our perspectives unique, and why these conversations matter. There's no one right way as far as living our lives. We get to do this in community with each other and we get to share experiences and knowledge. You have a gift of being able to look at it with fresh eyes, whereas this has been a lifelong journey for me. You have a fresher perspective which, I think, is especially useful as well. I love it.

I do, too. And I think we need more encouragement so that people can have conversations on faith no matter where they are on their faith journey. Sometimes we're tempted to think we can only seek out people who are brand-new or only able to dip in one toe if that's where we are. Maybe we think, "I don't want to really be surrounded or talk to people who are really strong and devout because I'm not there." However, I have learned that faith conversations are healing—those who are just beginning gain so much from those farther along. It works both ways. We need to meet people where they are and where we are, and not be ashamed.

For a long time, I did feel ashamed that I really didn't have much faith knowledge. I had a deep longing, but I didn't have a way to develop it or grow in my faith. I grew up in a great family, but faith was not at the center. And that's where it was and what it was. And I often wish I could have known God was there, sooner. But that was God's plan for me. Because I came to God truly in desperation, I'm open to saying, "Well, I'm new, this is new, that's just the way it is." And I can really learn so much from someone like you, Victoria, and from others who've been at this far longer and walked with God in a deeper way.

As I've gotten over myself a little, I've learned to be more open to sharing my story. And perhaps because of my story I can really see the practical application of so much scripture, because of what I've been through. I believe women can learn so much from each other if we only let it happen.

And that's the thing. At the end of the day, the key to all these conversations is to have vulnerability. We must pull the masks off. And I say this a lot and I write about this a lot. I'm beating my drum here. The reality is, if we are always saying we've got it all together, all figured out, we always look at other people and think they've got it together as well. You know this.

> *And after you have suffered a little while, the God of all grace, who has called you to his eternal glory in Christ, will himself restore, confirm, strengthen, and establish you.*
>
> *1 Peter 5:10*

We look at others and think, they know what they're doing. Everything's great. And the reality is, is we're all just a mess. None of us has everything completely figured out. We're all just trying to get by, you know. If we're honest with each other we'd say, you know what, I don't know what that means, or I don't know what to think about that. When there's not judgment on the receiving side, we can have open conversation and dialogue. We might say, maybe that's not quite right, or that is right, or that's something to think about.

You know, it's a beautiful thing. And that's how the body of Christ should be. It should be an open dialogue. It should not be, you don't know what you're talking about. It shouldn't be divisive. It shouldn't. So much of what we're doing is what I long for: for people to have friends they can discuss things with openly and honestly. My hope is that they can say, you know what, I don't have it all together.

I have a book coming out soon that will tell everybody I don't have it all together. There is some real risk there because I'm being open and saying, I've done this wrong a lot through the years. I've done this aspect of my walk wrong because I was afraid to let on that I didn't know what I was doing. And sometimes my motivations weren't always right. And I've had to learn through the process.

I'm sharing that so other people don't have to go through what I went through on their own. And so they will know they're not alone.

That's the key, nobody is alone. If you're reading this and you know a lot about scripture, you have something to add to the conversation, we're so happy to have you here. If you don't know anything about scripture, if you don't even own a Bible, please keep reading, because we've been there too.

God celebrates you, wherever you are on your journey. Maybe you've thought about reading the Bible but haven't gotten around to it or you've been intimidated. Perhaps you've heard criticism of the Bible in our culture. The corollaries in scripture to our modern lives are astounding. We hope you'll take the opportunity to be refocused on your journey with Jesus, meeting Him and the Father in the Bible, however it suits you best.

Wherefore seeing we also are compassed about with so great a cloud of witnesses, let us lay aside every weight, and the sin which doth so easily beset us, and let us run with patience the race that is set before us, Looking unto Jesus the author and finisher of our faith.

—Hebrews 12:1-2 KJV

ROTATING RENOVATION DREAM LIST

*discernment for today, and
again in a few weeks*

It's important to think about all the possibilities and let them live on paper somewhere. If you've experienced that sinking feeling of "I wish my house was different—*a lot different*—everywhere," **make your renovation dream list.** In words, not pictures, make a list of all the things you would do to the house if money were no object. Include improvements that would serve how you live, *right now*, better, but not fantasy projects. Date the list and revisit it in two months. At that time rewrite your list without looking at the original.

How we feel about the shortcomings of the house is always shifting based on the season we are in and the season of the year. Other influences include other homes we've seen recently and our mood at the time! It's helpful to do this exercise a few times, especially if you're gearing up for a big renovation. It's important to check your notes. Do you still want all those things? Is there anything you would change? Making a working list of projects requires reflection and observation—and noting which projects come up consistently. It's important that married couples work through this discernment process together (or separately but then "compare notes") and ultimately come to agreement on what projects would be best for the home.

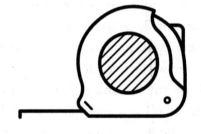

Chapter 8

REMADE

remade: /re mad/ *adjective*

to have been made anew, in a new form[1]

Having a Designer who cares to remake us is such an encouraging concept. While being remade in our hearts can be a challenging process, it is always worthwhile. When we remake things in our home, we bring the gifts God gives us to the process. He is truly with us in home-making or re-making!

The passage about the potter in Jeremiah gives us such a beautiful word picture for "remade." I love word pictures. I can envision exactly what is being said. I'm going to read the passage because I think it is so fascinating. This is from Jeremiah 18, and it says "The word which came to Jeremiah from the Lord saying arise and go down to the Potter's House. And there I will announce my words to you. Then I went to the Potter's House and there he was making

---

1   https://www.merriam-webster.com/dictionary/remade

something on the wheel. But the vessel that he was making of clay was spoiled in the hand of the potter. So, he remade it into another vessel as it pleased the potter to make." Just a few verses later, it said that the Lord was talking to Israel, and He said, "Behold, like the clay in the potter's hand. So are you in my hand house of Israel."

I just love that picture of the clay on the wheel and it not going well¬—which if I was doing clay on a wheel, I can assure you it will not go well. But in God's hands, we are remade and given a brand-new purpose without having to completely start over. So, I just love the idea of remade.

I have images of that 1980s movie, *Ghost*, in my mind now—but moving on—anyone who follows me on social media knows that I collect hands. I'm obsessed with hands. Hands are such a big part of our spiritual lives as well as our lives as makers, moms, caretakers, friends and wives. Hands are what we use to love and care for people and make things. And I'm obsessed with that vision of the Lord's hands at work on us—what a powerful, powerful image to help us grow in faith.

Every time I see hands in my house, I'm reminded that I'm sitting in the palm of His hand and His hands are at work when my hands fall short, which they do every day. This also calls to mind a big hunk of clay on the wheel, which is really ugly.

They call it a lump, right? Like this lump of nothing. Right? There's no shape.

Yes! There's no form. It's just a blob! And sometimes with a design project, you're walking into a blob. It might be a house covered in something that needs to be removed or you're walking into something in a very raw state. A customer of mine is in full-demo mode. So, we're seeing the very raw space. It's clay-like and we're seeing it come to life very slowly.

I think when we can invite God in—when we see our homes as the clay, we can invite God into our process. He's there if we're open to Him.

Absolutely. My personal belief is that God is not distant or far away. I really do believe that He cares about each one of us personally. I mean, the Bible is clear on this. He knows the number of hairs on our head. He sees our tears and he collects them in a bottle. These are very personal interactions He has with us, right? And so, I don't believe God is far off and thinks that whatever I'm doing in my home has nothing to do with Him.

All of it does—every part of my life. I don't compartmentalize my faith. It fills my life and encompasses everything. That's true in our homes as well when we remake a room or a space. We're part of that design and creative process, and He is the ultimate designer in creation. So, I think that's part of being in His image.

I'm so glad you said that, because in my coming to find and know God as an adult, I had to come to believe that God cared about me, including the most mundane details of my life. I had to start to believe He cared about my well-being and how I functioned throughout the day. I couldn't get there if I thought that God only cared about war, dramatic headline grabbing situations or the human condition as a whole. If I couldn't bring Him into my life and believe that He cared deeply for me, a solitary being out of 7 billion others on the planet, I wasn't going to make it. That was a sea change for me—understanding God cares for me. I was working with a friend in her dining room, and we were speculating about whether God really cared about her project. This is one of my most faithful friends, mind you, striving to make this room beautiful. I believed God had a plan for that dining room; to open it up and make of it a place, a shared table for our community. It's going to be more than just a space to contemplate, *do I like this wallpaper, or is this pretty or does God even care?* I think that He does care because God has a plan for our homes—beyond what we can even think or imagine.

I know you feel passionately about this—using spaces to love others. You've taught me this beautiful term, which I'd never heard before: *mission work.* Right? This is what we mean when we talk about giving the home a purpose and a beauty that extends well beyond the surface.

You're right, I do talk about that a lot. I think we miss how we could leverage our resources in a different way for Kingdom work and mission work for reaching out. For example, selecting storage items for different rooms in our home so that we can toss kids toys in rapidly when folks are coming in the door. We can quickly scooch through the room dumping things in a cube with a lid. You feel better knowing it doesn't look as crazy as it did earlier. Or planning the size of my dining table or the flow of my room to accommodate a crowd will make people feel welcome. I'm passionate about that. Don't get me going!

I know, I can't wait to come to your house! But we're remaking a space, not for Instagram or anyone's approval, but for the mission of our home. And God's in the mission and in the remaking—that's my soapbox, really! We're remaking a space in concert with God. That makes the whole work of the home more than just a flight of fancy. You know, when I was younger and I first said, "I think I want to be a decorator" out loud, I was a bit embarrassed. You see, when I was growing up, I thought decorating was vapid, not important enough to devote one's life to. I still harbor a bit of that. Sometimes I think we can make what we do vapid or meaningless, but we can also think about the home and all that goes into it as creating a sacred space and working on a mission. You never know where those conversations that take place in that dining room you've created will lead. You don't know what opening your home to somebody else means, let alone what the home will mean to your own family.

> *Return to your stronghold,*
> *O prisoners of hope;*
> *today I declare that I will*
> *restore to you double.*
>
> *Zechariah 9:12*

I don't feel like I am a great host. Yet I've had times in my life with people in my home that felt like there was something else other than me at work. The time we shared then created something new. Especially now when people are getting together, after being apart, it's even less about look and feel.

It's the simple things that matter the most. Now, it's not the elaborate functions or the most beautiful home. Everyone just desires being with someone, having a coffee or just conversation, a listening ear. I'm experiencing it. You're experiencing it. People are longing for relationships and relationships are built in the kitchen half the time! They're built around the ordinary, everyday experiences that have become extraordinary because we have all been so far apart for so long.

I'm finding that we have a true hunger for those connections that can be quite simple to fill. You do need a table and a chair. But you know what? You might not need what you thought you needed. For example, you might not need all the trappings your mom needed to have people over. What you need is to open your heart and let God do His work.

At this point I really do feel remade. I was that lump of clay. I'm really clear that my role is small, and, although I've evolved, I'm not even half-way in charge. My job is to let God guide me. "Thy will not mine be done." I'd love to be in charge, but I've learned to show up and say, *OK, what's Your will for me here, Lord?*

I love that being remade means in His image, we're created in His image. Yet we still fall short. We're not holy, not just and we're not merciful. We're not any of the things that are the character traits of God.

And yet He is still working on us! There's a whole process of sanctification, if we want to use the big word for it. He is making us new and taking all that junk from us if we let

Him. Also part of the process is being willing to be remade and become more like Him. That's my desire, to be more like Him. I want more of Him and less of me, because there's a lot of junk in me.

> We came across this beautiful bumper sticker that said, "He is greater than" but it was only the letters "H" and "E" and the greater-than sign. My kids squealed, "I know that from math class!" And I said, "well I'm glad you remember that!"

Yes, they're learning something!!

> Yes, thanks be to God! That bumper sticker reminded me of my spiritual roots. As I said earlier, I came to God through 12-step programs. To participate in those, you only need to adopt the most rudimentary explanation or understanding of God, which was a big step for me. You do not have to read the Bible, believe in capital-G - God. You don't have to say the word Jesus. You just need to believe that it's not *just you*—there's something bigger than you—a higher power. Some people in the program spend their whole life calling God a higher power. Others are drawn, as I was, to Jesus. I believe that early "God-concept" led me to Him. He was my higher power all along though I couldn't see it—and He was ok with being called "HP." But that was my kernel of truth—that it's not me in charge, which is the good and bad news. It's not all up to me and that is a huge relief.

I mean, it's very relieving to be able to say, it's not all up to me. It's not all on my shoulders. I think we carry a lot of unnecessary weight on our shoulders. It's not what I can do in my own power. And that is very freeing when we allow it.

Have you ever thought of yourself as needing to be remade? The beauty of the work Christ does in us is that He makes us new. We don't have to be better or try harder before we surrender. Rather we can come as we are, and He does the work. This is so freeing and so powerful. Do you feel remade? It's powerful to reflect in gratitude on all God's work in you that has already been accomplished.

The word that came to Jeremiah from the LORD: "Arise, and go down to the potter's house, and there I will let you hear my words." So I went down to the potter's house, and there he was working at his wheel. And the vessel he was making of clay was spoiled in the potter's hand, and he reworked it into another vessel, as it seemed good to the potter to do.

Then the word of the LORD came to me: "O house of Israel, can I not do with you as this potter has done? declares the LORD. Behold, like the clay in the potter's hand, so are you in my hand, O house of Israel.

—Jeremiah 18:1-6

Brothers, if anyone is caught in any transgression, you who are spiritual should restore him in a spirit of gentleness. Keep watch on yourself, lest you too be tempted.

Galatians 6:1

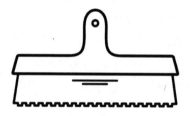

Chapter 9

REPURPOSED

repurposed: re/per/pes *adjective*

given a new purpose

*first known use, 1984[1]

Repurpose is a relatively modern word, first used in the early 1980s in the context of rebuilding old computers. It is a fashionable word in design today, with an ancient connection as we contemplate God's purpose for us and our humanity. Here we talk about using the good, bad and ugly, whether it's something you find at a thrift store or a challenging event that affects life and the house. Perhaps it is something that deserves to be repurposed for good.

A lot of conversation happens about items we have in our homes, especially when we're on a budget and shouldn't be spending or splurging. The verse I was drawn to about being

---

1   www.merriam-webster.com/definition/repurpose

repurposed is from Proverbs. I love Proverbs and the many salient, short and sweet pointers for daily living. Proverbs 19:21 says "many are the plans in a person's heart. But it is the Lord's purpose that prevails." And I thought, oh my, that is definitely where I am.

I always have lots of plans. I have lots of agendas and things. Ultimately, however, it's the Lord's purpose that matters and He repurposes my heart many times to go in a direction He has for me. That was where I was leaning when I thought about this conversation today. I'm going to toss it over to you, Paige, to talk about your thoughts on the word repurpose.

As you were reading, I was thinking it can't be an accident that all these words have incredible biblical meanings *and* incredible meanings in our home as well. Right? I don't just mean the home itself. We're talking about furniture, DIY projects, and all of the work of making a home and its interior design: everything from painting the front door to a $100,000 renovation. It can't be an accident that these two worlds are connected by these words—every word we talk about! I love the verse you read. I literally just made a note "read more Proverbs" because "short and impactful" is my jam. I'll take all those tips from you!

> *Lord, I have heard the report of you, and your work, O Lord, do I fear. In the midst of the years revive it; in the midst of the years make it known; in wrath remember mercy.*
>
> *Habakkuk 3:2*

I would say *repurpose* is a bit of a buzzword in design, because people love the idea of repurposing something cool or interesting in a new way. It is intriguing, repurposing a beloved tree as a table or barn wood elsewhere in the home. In terms of economics, we repurpose things all the time to save money. For instance, I have a customer who is gutting her kitchen. We're putting the old cabinets in the basement because they're in good condition and *waste not want not!* They no longer work in her kitchen, but there's no reason she can't use them elsewhere.

We don't talk about that enough. When I first started working in this business, there was all this talk about green stuff. What's green? What's eco-friendly? What's sustainable? What isn't? The reality is the greenest building strategy is to use what we have. The materials in your home may not be great for the environment. Yet, if you're using them over a long period of time, their longevity will benefit you and your family. And that is very green, actually! It's constant consumption and demolition—all those materials going to the landfills—that is unsustainable. Unsustainable is throwing out what still works.

A few years ago, I was asked by a few companies if I would give a talk on green building. After my presentation they would say, "That's not what we had in mind. We thought you were going to promote our bamboo flooring." I would respond, "I'm so sorry but I actually think if your flooring is fine, you shouldn't replace it at all." My company sponsored speaking career was short!

But I also love the idea of contemplating our life's purpose. We have our idea of our purpose or plan—perhaps we expect to have a certain house, live a certain way, or to have a certain family. And then God comes in and, because we're dependent on God's will for our children, things might look quite different. I think our vision for our life as adults needs to be open because things don't always turn out our way. The home certainly reflects that, which can be painful.

Sometimes we buy a house that's too big, or one that's too small. We realize this later and we either enlarge our space by knocking out walls or rent out the surplus room over the garage. You make adjustments.

This week I talked to a class of college students pursuing their major studies about purpose and how things change. How many people actually continue doing what they majored in for the rest of their lives? The decisions you make when you're younger are not all going to work necessarily. Sometimes you've got to repurpose and replan what you're going to do, and that's OK. The hardest thing for some people is to be flexible. Still, I love the idea. You talked about wood repurposed for a table. I have a dear client who had a massive tree fall in her yard after a hurricane. It was just huge.

A part of it was made into a table. Talk about a piece that enables you to have conversations about it forever! She had just been on the porch that was crushed by that tree. Her dog needed her attention, and she was drawn away just before the tree fell. She now has this amazing story to relate and this beautiful piece of furniture from this crazy, massive tree.

Something devastated their home and had to be dealt with, but there's something of lasting beauty left afterward.

> Oh my gosh, talk about a story of being saved! I just love that—it really speaks to my heart. Building upon tragedy, trial or challenge in the home and keeping something from it reminds me of an odd story.

Before our kids came along, my husband and I traveled a lot. We made an Eastern European trek and found ourselves in the city of Sarajevo, Bosnia. It wasn't exactly dangerous, but also not cushy and comfortable either. Sarajevo was a war-torn city with vestiges of the war still visible. They did something unique: where mortar shells exploded in the street (the conflict happened in the early 1990s), they painted the hole red. They call these "Sarajevo Roses," and keep them as memorials to the war; a reminder of what happened there. We were there in the early 2000s and this happened in the last 10-15 years. I bring that story up to say, sometimes things happen and we're eager to cover them up. A flood or a tree falling into the home, that's a house which obviously needs to be fixed.

However, there's another approach when something happens to us, we give ourselves a chance to keep a piece of it in some way. You might have held on to something of a loved one no longer with us. Many of my clients have something from a parent who's passed away. They'll say, "I need to do something with this piece. I don't know what to do with it, but let's keep it. I want to keep it in front of my face." They want to use these objects, not out of obligation to the person who has passed, but as a memento of that person that lives on in their home, perhaps in an entirely new way. Each home could have something like that. It's about the journey we've been on and what we've overcome or someone who's left us.

I just love that.

Yes, it's the remembrance. It's being able to tell the story and story is important. Everyone has stories, and everyone has something worth value to share with someone else.

That could be an encouragement. That could be an inspiration. We've all had difficult experiences and when we share that with someone else, there's a bond that's created in that shared experience. And then there's hope. Of all the things we need right now, the most important may well be massive amounts of hope. There are so many people who are struggling, and having new purpose gives hope. There's more to life out there.

Should you have a piece of furniture or some things left from that experience to help you tell the story, you can share with someone else and be an encouragement. We can say, it was awful at the time. It really was awful, just as having a relative go through cancer is awful. Yet there's always hope because then I can share how we made it.

I think we encourage others to not only open up, but express things of life that are not necessarily the bright spots. I talk a lot about using memories or colors from your favorite vacations and drawing from cherished experiences. In reality, our stories are more than rainbows and picture-perfect vacations. Those make our personal highlight reel and part of our story. On the other hand, I have art in my house which depicts some of the worst parts of my life.

You might ask, why would you want that up?

I can't explain it other than to say there's some art that just touches me. It reminds me of a hard time that is no longer here anymore. That's powerful for me to appreciate that the hard time is indeed in the past and God walked me through. That is immensely powerful. I could have things that only remind me of the present loveliness, but that's not the whole of who I am. Our stories, as you said, are so powerful for ourselves, let alone others who might ask, "what's up with that?"

> *After two days he will revive us; on the third day he will raise us up, that we may live before him.*
>
> *Hosea 6:2*

Let me tell you, this artist reminds me of some of my darkest days. She reminds me of me! She's a dark soul, very troubled, and I see myself in her—even if it isn't evident to you. This is a reminder that God's given us a purpose and He has repurposed us. In many ways our journey is about being repurposed and changed for something better.

When you were talking about that verse at the start it reminded me of my career. I really wanted to be an interior designer. I was very focused on a certain kind of work. I lived in New York City and did certain kinds of projects. I felt disenfranchised and moved out of the city. I wanted to do different kinds of projects. It was then I started to think about inviting God into my work. I decided that I couldn't continue to do this unless my faith was a big part of it, which doesn't work for everybody. Yet I didn't feel I could ignore that. This became my vision for my career; being more open to God's call and His will for me. That's what really comes up with this word today.

We're not in charge of the work He sets before us. As I go through my day, I can see many possibilities for going different directions, professionally. I can visualize merely talking about the home in strictly design terms, never addressing the soul and the journey. I can see that as an option for someone else, but I can't do it anymore. That's not the path for me.

I love that. The crux of being repurposed is understanding this may not have been the original plan. Consider repurposing items, furniture or a space in our home to be more accommodating. That wasn't the original plan although it's what we need now. It's the right thing for us at this moment and in this day.

When we talk about plans as it relates to our spiritual life, God's always got a better plan than mine. It's always a better plan. Again, this fills me with such hope! I don't like change. I don't. I like to set it, forget it and never mess with it again. I am a girl that dislikes change.

Change can be uncomfortable; I prefer to be ready for it or planning it. And I'm not always, but that's what God is teaching me. He's stretching me. He's moving me in new ways and repurposing my steps. This involves change and acceptance of it. But what's funny is I know you love change which makes us polar opposites.

I'm definitely a change addict! As you're talking, I'm thinking about your beautiful screens. I would have painted them five different colors by now! Even though they are amazing in gold, and they should never be anything but gold, I would have made them black, white and maybe pink, without a doubt.

At least you tried. You won't know what you like until you try it. And I know—I know! But I just can't change sometimes!

I think we arrive at the same place eventually. I want to be in charge of all the changes and have a final say regarding anybody *else's* change. I want to be in charge with my finger on the button. Any change is mine. It's two sides of the same coin!

It's still a control thing!

Yes. Hopefully the older I get; I am growing in flexibility and openness to other people's approaches and input. That slows me down a bit, too. You know, God speaks to us in many different ways.

If God can use a donkey to talk to Balaam[2], I'm pretty sure he can use most anything to get our attention.

There's no end to talking about change and being repurposed and plans and what God has for us. We hope that you are encouraged that God can and will "repurpose" your steps for your future no matter what has happened in your life or where you feel stuck! Do you suspect God is guiding you to a different purpose than your current work? Can you take this to prayer, journaling or your quiet time with the Lord, this week?

Many are the plans in a person's heart, but it is the LORD's purpose that prevails.

—*Proverbs 19:21 NIV*

2 See the Book of Numbers, Chapter 22 for this incredible story!

LOST IN A RAINBOW

The wall of colors at the paint store is mind-numbing, Pinterest has zillions of ideas of greys and neutrals that work "anywhere" yet you desperately want to add color to your home. But which one? If you're hiring a painter, you feel compelled to get it right the first time. I get that. I suggest a "sample pot" 12oz or so that you can easily paint on the wall to test a color. If you're not sure which color to even begin considering, remember *your real life*. Think about where you like to be or vacation. Think about the colors of favorite foods. Visit your closet. Connect the color of your choice to your own life and the project will be quite different for you. If you are struggling to determine which color or colors to choose for a piece of furniture, or a whole room, pick a color from the pallet of your life. I worked with a client who wore green constantly, had a green car and a green phone case. It was a slam dunk that we would use the green hue that was everywhere in her life, for her bathroom renovation! Don't be led astray by "trendy" colors—use what is in your life already—color is deeply personal. When the project feels personal, it will have a greater impact on you. To make your choice of color, purchase sample pots of three colors (no more), paint a square foot (literally 12"x12") either directly on the wall or on white posterboard and use that to guide you. Do not look at paint colors side-by-side—your eyes will work against you. Look at each color independently. Give yourself a deadline but, as the Bible says, "be not afraid."

Chapter 10

RENAMED

renamed[1]: /re-nam-ed/ *adjective*

given a new name

Have you ever wondered about the origins of your name, or why something has a particular name? Have you wished that you could change your name or the label someone has maybe given you or worse that you have given yourself? Be encouraged, friends! You are more than the label or name you've been given!

I feel a soap box moment coming on with this word "renamed." People who know me know I have a thing with labels and design buzzwords and the like. I don't know if I should start hot and heavy like that!

Well, I know. Let's talk about spiritual applications and then we can talk about the home. The spiritual concept of adoption

---

1 Rename | Definition of Rename by Merriam-Webster (merriam-webster.com)

is brought up in the Bible and relates to being renamed. We're adopted as sons and daughters of God when we are brought into his family through salvation. That is a beautiful thing to think about; being renamed. It's a new identity. You brought up this new identity conversation a little while ago.

Yes. The first time I was part of a Bible study was a few years ago, when my kids were babies. And I remember being addressed as a "daughter of Christ," a child of God. I had never considered that before. It was a new identity, one that had been foreign to me. I have chills even saying that because it's a concept that makes me feel loved and dignified, taken care of, wanted and intended.

There's a lot of meaning in that name, in the word daughter. There is a lot of power in it. When we need to be lifted up, the knowledge that God wanted us as his adopted children is very powerful. In that same study, I learned, and please correct me if I'm wrong, that adoption in biblical times, bestowed important rights. One could legally disown their birth child, but never an adopted child. The fact that God uses the language of adoption is very meaningful. And it's on purpose!

It's absolutely on purpose. I agree. Understanding that use of language is important. I also enjoy studying the meaning of names. It's interesting the names we give our children. When you examine the meaning of those names, some names don't convey much. However, some say a great deal. This may be especially true whenever we're named after a relative or given a family name which has been passed down from generation to generation.

I love thinking about the meaning of names. Victoria means victorious spirit. Many people use the short-form Vicki which means "leader." And you know I like to be in charge.

As I am a creative person, I wanted to invent new names for my children! We're going to literally invent words with letters that have never been combined that way. I wanted a whole new identity for them. I also married into a family where everyone is named after someone else and I thought, "we're not going to do that."

I looked at my husband who is very outdoorsy. He loves outdoor places in Colorado and points west, and I was picking names from maps! "I think we should name our child after Bryce Canyon, Hon! Kanyon with a K. What do you think?"

In my first pregnancy I had a medical complication. My father-in-law, Frank, God rest his soul, was the most incredible man. He showed me such tenderness and grace as he helped us navigate the issue. He had a passion for helping people and he shared his wife's medical journey. (My husband had lost his mom just before we met.) He then advised me with such generosity. This was someone taking time out of their day to minister to me in my time of trial. I was facing the prospect of a blood transfusion and had decisions to make. It was nerve racking. He was on the road, but he pulled over and talked

> *Will you not revive us again, that your people may rejoice in you?*
>
> *Psalm 85:6*

me through this. When I hung up I was so relieved. I turned to my husband and said, "I want to name our son, Francis Xavier, after your dad." I wanted my son to be like his father's dad. He exemplified selflessness, love and service right there on the highway. We couldn't have two guys in the house named Francis, so my son goes by Xavier. It is meaningful to me that my son and my father-in-law became connected in that act of service.

That's so beautiful! Just as being renamed when God takes hold of us and gives us a new identity. That is a beautiful story in itself. Spiritually, it's just beautiful. Yet worrying about names in our homes can be a little difficult.

I know you have a passion about this, so talk to me about style names and the vocabulary.

Deep breaths...I struggle...First, I think a lot of the style labels for the home are literally manufactured, produced by marketers for the big furniture manufacturers and makers of decorative items. These companies decide what modern or boho or farmhouse is. Yet they frequently assign these labels on a whim, related to almost no truth. That bothers me! Then there are many people who say, "I like (a certain) style," which they wear like a strait jacket. Now we're constricted and can only put things in their home drawn from that style. And as I have noted, their "style" is a word used rather loosely by marketers.

I understand some people need rules and order in their home. I have more eclectic taste, so I feel very free to borrow from almost any design legacy or era. However, we can get stuck on labels and names. I invite people to be curious about certain names or styles—even if they aren't particularly drawn to them. The true history of these traditions is fascinating; the origin story of modern design is fascinating!

At the dawn of the 20th century, some people wanted to try life without any detail, artifice, ornamentation. They wanted to strip things down to their simplest forms in architecture, consumer goods and homes as a reaction to political and social mores where formality, artifice and ornate design had been the status quo. And that's where modern design came from—a desire to unearth utility, beauty and simplicity in materials which modernists saw as buried. I get excited about this! People refer to all manner of things in the marketplace as "modern" and I have to scream inside my head, "that's not modern!" They've taken to slapping that label on anything not apparent as something else and really misusing it. Perhaps I become too academic and excited by the subject, but I have always been curious about names and terms in design. Look at how we change the names for furniture constantly—is it a bureau or a dresser? Is it an armoire or a console? Is it a credenza? Depends on the store! There is a lot of variation.

But what is the right answer? Does it depend on where you live?

It's regional! Sometimes furniture definitions are rigid, for example that of a highboy, but I don't want people to get lost in that. Instead let us be clear what our needs and desires are for a particular piece and then discern what we like. There are no "style" police who will come to your home and say, "That should have been a credenza, but you chose a console!" The most important thing is to use what you like

regardless of different style names. Names in our business
really mislead consumers.

People get confused by names. I have a theory. At this stage
I don't know if it's true or not. Anecdotally, I have noticed
furniture marketers, in concert with big data, use the names
of places where we live or vacation, or names we've used in
online searches to name their furniture. I live in Kensington
and I've seen lots of things named Kensington marketed to me!

I guess a familiar word gives us comfort and a connection
with a piece. Marketers know people are lost in the sea of
options online!

Yeah, I like that. I don't think there's any furniture
called Nesbit.

If you do see that though, you'll confirm my suspicion!

If Wayfair comes out with a Nesbit something, we'll know!

I'm going to look for it!

You're right. Kensington is definitely a name used for
different groups, not necessarily different styles, of furniture.
Things share that name.

The old-fashioned term of chifforobe is still technically a
thing. It had drawers and space to hang garments.

But everybody calls that an armoire now. It's all the
same, right?

Right! There are generational shifts and changes also. My
grandparents used to refer to certain things differently—is
it a divan? Is it a sofa? Some of the words are fun. I like
the old terminology and I have some great old furniture
encyclopedias I love to look through. The problem is when
we get hung up and feel our space must contain this china
cabinet because that is the rule, rather than focusing on what
we or our families need.

It can feel overwhelming, keeping up with it all. There is the
fear, running rampant, that our things are timely or of the
moment, chic or in, and if I don't get that "right," I'm going
to be "out." I wish I could take that fear away from everybody.

I can appreciate a lot of different things, but they don't all
necessarily go together well in a home. You must have a bit of
a discerning eye but that doesn't mean you have to be locked
into "only macramé and green plants!"

Oh dear, the macrame...This speaks to homogenization. I
was listening to an interview and the people were talking
about how many images of people's homes we see these days
on social media. You're looking more at pictures of homes,
today, than had you subscribed to five shelter magazines
20 years ago!

Despite that, we're seeing so much homogeneity, the same
stuff repeatedly. Part of that is due to our tribal nature.
We like what this person has and so that's what we want.

This leads to such rigidity it distorts the original spirit of a particular style. Don't get me started on "boho." I studied in the Czech Republic and I'm very protective of my Bohemia, which has been extrapolated and connected to boho. We misuse the term, and to the point now it's only plants and macramé, which is a bummer. I could take another 45 minutes to discuss that, but nobody wants to hear it. When a style becomes a straitjacket, it becomes a set of rules that people merely try to mimic. They see something in their chosen style that they've pledged allegiance to, and they say, "I want to buy that exact rug." With social media and current purchase apps, you can buy someone's whole room if they have achieved the level of boho you think is cool.

It's better to be curious and open to a wider range. Whether you like what you've seen in magazines or Instagram, look at *everything*. If you say you hate modern, I challenge you to find influencers and designers actually devoted to a modern aesthetic.

And if you really love modern styles, I challenge you to subscribe to *Veranda* and other magazines with a totally different aesthetic and just objectively look. All this spurs creativity. If you're looking at the same thing all the time, you will feel bound to a set of rules. Then, you may think to yourself, "I'd like to paint my cabinets pink." But, if nobody else does that in my lane, you assume it's wrong.

"I don't see any pink cabinets in farmhouses." Well, perhaps you'll be the first one! Taking more risks makes this journey more enjoyable.

Well, it's being an original, right? There's nothing wrong with being an original—we are all unique. It's great to have something as a guide to give you ideas and inspiration. But at some point, definitely be you!

> In your hospitality book,[2] you have a primer on different styles, which is important. People need to have words to attach to what they like. This is what we call "eclectic." This is called "rustic modern," and, by the way, there are new terms all the time!

There are so many!

> When you search a website that sells a lot of things there may be 45 different styles to choose! Rustic, eclectic, modern, bohemian, and they're all mingled together with Scandinavian, etc. It's interesting to find the words attached to something you like. You may look at Scandinavian and think, "I like this. The white floors are cool! I may never do it, but I like it!"

It's interesting to learn and try to understand the why behind design disciplines. White floors are favored in Sweden due to their extremely long winters! It's dark out for months. White floors repel the darkness. Knowledge can be beneficial. Perhaps these aesthetic elements could function for you where you live! Education is important, but not to be bound

---

2 Extraordinary Hospitality for Ordinary Christians: A Radical Approach to Preparing Your Heart & Home for Gospel Centered Community. Good Books, 2020.

by what you discover. It is not ironclad. Even if you don't like plants, you can still draw from the bohemian tradition!

Sometimes a big part of my job is giving someone permission to keep something important to them. I have clients who tell me, "I have this outmoded piece. I should get rid of it, but I just can't." 99% of the time I'll say, "Let's keep it! We can work it in!" I'm pleased to hear someone say *I love this*. That is a beautiful thing. Or should they say, "I don't know, or I don't particularly care about this. I think it's dated," then I'm fully on board: "It certainly is!"

If they love it, of course we'll use it. We all know if you wait long enough, it'll be back in style again anyway.

Right! Things always come back around. Hello, 1980s!

Yes, mauve everywhere! Unbelievable!

This cracks me up.

"The Golden Girls" would be Instagram influencers right now with their Boca Raton home. If they had an Instagram page, it would be blowing up.

Shocking. I thought we had said "Adios" but here we are!

I know...pale pink, pale gray, oy!

I love how the concept of adoption is precious to us as believers. Being adopted by Christ and united into His family brings much joy and hope. Being renamed removes labels, removes fear and shame, and brings restoration. In our projects we can get hung up on style names. If this happens, go back to the *what* of the space—what happens here and what do we want to happen here? Coming back to our reason helps us wade through terms and into clarity.

For you did not receive the spirit of slavery to fall back into fear,
but you have received the Spirit of adoption as sons, by whom
we cry, "Abba! Father!" The Spirit himself bears witness with
our spirit that we are children of God, and if children, then
heirs—heirs of God and fellow heirs with Christ, provided we
suffer with him in order that we may also be glorified with him.

—Romans 8:15

Create in me a pure heart, O God, and renew a steadfast spirit within me. Do not cast me from your presence or take your Holy Spirit from me. Restore to me the joy of your salvation and grant me a willing spirit, to sustain me.

Psalm 51:10-12 NIV

Chapter 11

RECOVERED

recovered: /ri-ke-ver[1] *adjective*

1: the state of being returned or brought back to normal condition, archaic: RESCUE

2: made up for, gained by legal process

3: found or identified again, saved from loss, restored to usefulness: RECLAIMED

Recovered is a word full of meaning and many layers. This word has a very light and airy and exciting home project connotation. In a deeper way, it applies to our hearts being covered by the protection of God in our lives. For some of us, being *re-covered* when we've fallen, is a lifelong journey, one we'll explore here as well.

When recovering furniture, we hope the bones, or the structure, of the sofa or chair are still good. Perhaps the

---

1   Recover | Definition of Recover by Merriam-Webster (merriam-webster.com)

cover itself has gotten old or worn down by kids or stained by spills. Or it may be frayed or merely out of date. But, without spending a ton of money, you can freshen it up and make it better. Recovering furniture is not that expensive.

It's not! Recovering is one of my favorite things to employ. I've made a lot of DIY converts this way because it's *so* simple and empowering. Once you've taken an old chair and made it prettier with fabric of your choosing and a staple gun, there's no going back. Just as you said, it's very economical. Also, there is a lot of creative freedom in *you* choosing that fabric. Staplers are not very expensive and they're fun to use.

The law of the Lord is perfect, reviving the soul; the testimony of the Lord is sure, making wise the simple.

Psalm 19:7

Often when I'm working with someone, they will have a fear of making a mistake or buying materials they're not going to like. Add to this a fear of being stuck with unwanted results in their home. I remind them "You're not stuck, because if you want to change it again, *you change it again.*" Fabric remnants are not expensive. You can always go back to the old version. I've ripped stuff out and used it again elsewhere. You can begin with a dining room seat or an upholstered seat elsewhere. These go quickly and easily but then you could move on to doing a whole chair.

And of course, some chairs are simpler, some harder. Many YouTube tutorials teach the process of reupholstery. Recovering items with fabric is a gateway drug; let's put it that way!

And then there's peel-and-stick wallpaper. I mean, that's a game changer. You can love a variety of patterns and have something different each time you use it. These are not permanent changes.

Peel-and stick-paper wallpaper, and the accompanying printing technology are amazing. It's incredible how many choices we have and how sophisticated the technology has become. And as you said, it's easy. Working with traditional wallpaper is not overly hard but is labor intensive. Any kind of papering gives you that sense of incorporating your personality and doing it yourself. You'll feel empowered whether you change it out, or something messes it up or you change your mind. It's all experience.

You can use these printed vinyl adhesive papers to cover the back of a piece of furniture or a section of wall. A piece of furniture can be covered magically. We're not talking about high skill DIY. There are no power tools. We're talking about fingertips, a ruler, and maybe a level. Empowering is really the word. You feel great doing it.

I think it's funny you mentioned fingertips, because if a hot glue gun is involved, I lose multiple fingertips in the process. Give me a staple gun instead. That's much better. Slipcovers remind me there are simple things that can be done to improve our homes quickly without a huge labor cost. If we're tired of seeing something and want to replace it, we don't need to break the budget. Even if we are just not ready to commit, we can recover something fairly quickly.

I'm reminded of the verse in Psalms of how we're covered with His feathers. Psalm 91:4 is one of my favorite verses because it depicts taking refuge under God's wings. It's a beautiful word picture of being protected. Sometimes slipcovers will protect from kids, spills, and other things. Covering reminds me, perhaps it's not a re-cover, but a covering of protection.

> I love that, too, because when you have small children, or your home gets used a lot, or maybe something's taken outside—it's true freedom to enjoy it knowing it can't be ruined beyond help or that it can be cleaned if necessary. I love the image of being under God's wing. That's beautiful.

> In the beginning of this chapter, Victoria, you spoke of a piece of furniture having good bones despite the outside being a bit shabby. That speaks to me because I feel like I was that piece of furniture, that person that needed a lot of work. I was a true rehab! But something there was redeemable. God knew that. I've had the word "recovery" in the back of my mind because it's such a big part of my personal story.

It is an important part of your story. It is what makes you, you. It also relates to many people who are in the same situation or face similar things with family.

> Right. Yet this isn't really the place for a deep dive into my story, I'd need a couple hours for that! I came to know God through my utter brokenness and due to being a sensitive

young person who felt that deep emptiness I now know was a God-sized hole. I tried to fill that hole with many things: food, alcohol, spending, relationships and various dysfunctional behaviors, seeking solace, comfort and unity. None of these fit the bill—they came up short every time. Ultimately, there's only one answer for that longing and that hunger. Ironically, the word hunger is so apt, and it really is hunger for God. I still wake up with that hunger and that ache. I know better now. I have better tools and I'm better equipped to answer that yearning.

It's a lifetime journey. Even folks who have never experienced different addictions or compulsive behaviors can relate to that ache and not knowing what to do with it. And they, too, sometimes pick something up that isn't good for us. The idea of recovering one day at a time and growing in our walk with God one day at a time is beautiful. Just as an old piece of furniture needs a lot of work, we also are getting there, slowly but surely.

That's the story. Ultimately, we're saying we are not perfect in and of ourselves. We're not any better than anybody else. We put ourselves out there and say, God, take our good bones, or bad bones, whatever we have and shape us into your best. This can only happen with His help.

For you that all began with addiction. For many of us it was recovery from hurts, habits, issues or hang ups we all have. This year has given us lots of fodder for that. I think we all need God to rescue us. That was what was fascinating about looking into verses as we were approaching this chapter on recovery. So many verses popped up with the theme of rescue. While not specifically using the word recovery, most dealt with the rescue Jesus brought into our lives. That was such a beautiful picture for me also, that recovery really is about rescue. Furthermore, it is, to me, ultimately redeeming that because we tell our stories for a reason, we go through experiences for a reason.

I believe wholeheartedly this may be the reason I can help someone in the future. I can walk alongside them and say, I've been down this road and it's not pretty or easy. But there's hope, there's a brighter tomorrow. I know what this looks like. I know what you're facing because when we feel seen, we feel known. We feel somebody understands who we are.

You mentioned this in connections with meetings and somebody knowing your name.

Yes. There's a story in the gospel of Mark[2] about Jesus driving a demon out of this poor, naked man, who's broken out of his chains and shackles. He was just struggling in many different ways. As a person with an addictive past, I can relate to trying a lot of things to try to fix yourself before you arrive at the solution. And when he comes to Jesus, the Lord simply says,
what is your name?

I still get choked up thinking about this. It's powerful to finally acknowledge what's going on with your addiction, with alcoholism, with over-eating. For me that moment came when I said, "Hi, my name is Paige and I'm here and I'm in this recovery community." I'm not saying this to a professional.

---

2   This beautiful story is in the Gospel of Mark, chapter 5.

I'm saying it to other people that are just like me. These are people who know what I am saying, are known in that way and know it themselves. This is very powerful.

In that particular story, Jesus tells the man he's completely cured. Onlookers are frightened by how *different* this man became following his encounter with Jesus. Jesus directs him to "go home and tell your family what happened." I don't feel a need to shout my story from the rooftops, but I do think God expects me to share my story. Potentially there's somebody out there seeking recovery for themselves or someone in their family. That's really the purpose of getting well, not cash or prizes. It's so that I can be more useful to my Creator.

> *You who have made me see many troubles and calamities will revive me again; from the depths of the earth you will bring me up again.*
>
> *Psalm 71:20*

Often part of that ache is not knowing what the purpose, or the meaning of our life is. To be more useful to my Creator is the sum purpose of my recovery. It has been a journey— something you can connect with doing too much of the "wrong" thing or not enough of the "right thing." Or simply not doing what's good for you, over and over again. I don't know anyone who can't relate to that.

Absolutely. What you said reminds me of the verse from Galatians 5:1 "Freedom is what we have because Christ has set us free. And stand then as free people and don't allow yourselves to become slaves again." So, we have freedom in Christ. Just as He set that man free from being demon-possessed, he has set us free from whatever entangles us.

That could be, as you said, a variety of things that hold us back from living out our purpose. It's a beautiful thing to be set free and to know our position in Christ is freedom. Once we have Christ, our position is freedom. If we go back, we chose to do that. I just love the truth of that because it is something we can hold on to, be anchored by and be grateful for. As you said that story helps encourage others.

> It does and it means now we need to share what we've been given. I think that's one of the reasons I'm here. I'm also thinking back to our analogy about recovering that old chair. Sometimes when you're trying to solve a problem within yourself, you're going to need to pick out a pretty fabric and put it right on.

You live with that for a while. And things have improved a lot by just getting a bit of recovery. For myself however, I had to peel that cover off and go deeper—deeper perhaps because more things need attention. That might require the cushion or foam be replaced or even the wood structure might be rotted. When you're ready, you'll want to look deeper inside relationships. You'll have to confront old hurts, grievances, tendencies (we call them "character defects") or things in you that caused problems with others. And you'll spend time just healing. You're not casting out these items like a demon, it's work that takes time and energy. We undertake working daily on ourselves and those very human parts of ourselves that have created conflict and problems in our lives. And it's done in community.

Somebody said to me, "isn't that a self-help group?" I'm not certain what that means, but I do know that 12-step recovery is, at its core, Christian, because it is about community and lifting each other up. It works, in part, because we're not all crazy at the same time. We lift each other up when we're in a good place and we reach out to others when we're not. Connection is a huge part of recovery, and from this comes holy friendship—friends who can call us out, hold us accountable. "Iron sharpens iron" We end up having friends who can actually talk about the real substance of life—just as we're doing here! Friendship and healthy conversation are a huge part of this journey to getting better.

We're made to live in community and that's where we grow. That means ripping off the facades and not being fake with people. It means being honest. When we are, we find real relationships and healing. If you need help in a particular area, do you have someone in your life that you can share this with? This may not be the person who actually provides help but sharing our need and desire for healing is truly the first step.

He will cover you with his feathers, and under his wings you will find refuge; his faithfulness will be your shield and rampart.

—Psalm 91:4 NIV

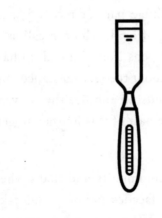

CLAIMING A BEAUTIFUL SPOT TO PRAY

a fixed or moveable feast

I personally don't care for the expression "prayer corner" because I don't think prayer should be relegated to the corner. I prefer to pray way out in the open! If you wish to devote space for quiet prayer and scripture reading, your needs are simple. Start with a comfortable chair, adequate light, space for your Bible and other spiritual books or devotionals and freedom from distractions. You can create a "kit" in a basket which can travel as needed or you can adapt a space you're already using—one that may have other functions through-out the day. A while ago, an organizer helped me create a dedicated prayer corner in my kitchen, without realizing it. Even though she wasn't particularly religious, she encouraged me to keep things in this corner that I found beautiful and were connected to what I did in this space. And what I did was to pray and read scripture early in the day before anyone woke up. She encouraged me to move or store everything else including an impressive cake stand collection. (I don't even bake!) She encouraged a singular focus for this little corner, even though it was used by others throughout the day. It was OK to claim it for my morning time with God. That was good advice—because even when I'm not sitting there, I'm remind-ed of our Lord every time I look at it—longing for 5am to come again! If you need permission to make space in your homes for your faith and growing with the Lord, here it is!

Appendix

REAL RECOVERY EXPLAINED: ADDITIONAL THOUGHTS & RESOURCES ON ADDICTION RECOVERY

You may have read about my recovery story in Chapter 11 and thought, "this is what I want:" freedom from a substance or behavior that has taken over your life. Perhaps you want this for a loved one or perhaps yourself. This first inkling, this desire for freedom, is the seed of recovery. Healing from addictions and compulsions is a lifelong journey, but the good news is, the work is rewarding even beyond the healing. God will use your recovery to bless others.

There are questions (FAQs) on every website for 12-step programs for people curious about themselves and their loved ones. *Am I an alcoholic? Am I addicted to porn? Am I a compulsive overeater? Am I addicted to self-harm?* I've put together a list of programs I am familiar with below. There are others not mentioned here and more are being developed all the time to meet that need, that hunger for God. Man tries to answer that hunger with things, behaviors, or substances. Addiction is not a moral failing—it is a disease and there is help.

There are many recovery programs and approaches to consider. The 12-step program format might not be appropriate for you or your loved one. What follows is a primer on the basics of 12-step programs so that you can familiarize yourself with how they work. Before I go any further, understand that the foundation of anonymous 12-step programs is the meeting. These are meetings where people gather (in person, online or by telephone) in an organized way to study recovery literature associated with the program, share their experiences and connect with one another. I'd suggest you try a meeting, if you're curious, to see if the program is right for you. That first meeting is not easy for anyone, but all of us who've experienced healing and long-term recovery have been there.

All anonymous 12-step programs are patterned after the original, Alcoholics Anonymous, founded in the United States in the 1930s. This program was founded by an alcoholic and a doctor—"Bill W." and "Dr. Bob." It has Judeo-Christian roots but remains a non-denominational program, open to all. People are not asked to believe in God if they don't care to. We do not mention Jesus and there are no scriptures in any of the literature for any 12-step program. Atheists, agnostics, even those who are hostile to religion are welcomed with open arms. The only requirement is a desire to stop drinking, using, or participating with one's drug of choice.

Step 1 is simply about admitting powerlessness. Step 2 is about acknowledging that there is a power greater than ourselves that can help us—we are not the only ones in the game, and we can find power outside ourselves. Step 3 asks us to turn our affliction and our life over to that power which is greater than ourselves. These three essential steps have been reduced to: I can't, God can, and I choose to let God. People who decide to work a 12-step program are invited to come up with a concept of a higher power (as mentioned in Step 2) any way they choose. When I went to my first meeting, I was angry and resentful of organized religion. I doubted God could or would do anything for me. When I looked at how powerless I was to control myself with regard to alcohol, food, my spending, my work, or relationships, I realized that there must be something out there more powerful than I. I came to believe there was a higher power at work in my life who cared for me. At first, my higher power was the group. These were strangers from all walks of life who understood exactly where I was when I attended my first meeting. I couldn't believe the love these people showed me until I responded the same way to a newcomer months later.

Recovery is hard, daily work that often asks people to reassess and rewrite their lives in profound ways. None of this happens right away, or quickly. It's a one-day-at-a-time process. For those in the early stages of recovery, it can be an hour- or a-moment-at-a-time situation.

The program is also one of intense personal reflection. Once "clean" and able to put down our substance or behavior, we begin the real work—healing old wounds, hurts and working on ourselves in earnest. Over time, Jesus invited me to go deeper into my Christian faith, deeper into a relationship with Him, deeper into self-understanding. I needed ten years of recovery before I was ready for that. Fortunately, God meets people where they are. It's my belief that He wants us to be well more than anything. Getting well and being able to be of service to another person still suffering (the primary purpose of the program) are ways of worshiping God, as I see it. We aren't able to worship Him when we aren't well—when our substances or behaviors replace God.

There are also programs for family members, spouses and others whose love binds them to addicts and alcoholics. These programs offer healing to folks in relationships with those in recovery. The solution isn't that different from the path to recovery for the addict—it's about letting go and letting God. One such program is affectionately called "Alanon."

Addiction is a devastating family problem that touches many people beyond the addict who sufferers by his own hand. There is hope however for recovery, and God wants this for every one of us.

Here are links to websites for major programs I am familiar with so that you can find a meeting in your area, or one online you can attend from wherever you live. Although there were zoom and telephone meetings prior to 2020, in most areas of the US, traditional face-to-face meetings transitioned to zoom or virtual meetings, and many have remained that way.

Alcoholics Anonymous: www.aa.org
Overeaters Anonymous: www.oa.org
Food Addicts Anonymous: www.foodaddictsanonymous.org
Narcotics Anonymous: www.na.org
Sex & Love Addicts Anonymous: www.slaafws.org
Nicotine Addicts Anonymous: www.nicotine-anonymous.org
Gamblers Anonymous: www.gamblersanonymous.org